D0847293

DATE DUE

MAR 1 5 1976

NOV 2 4 2004

THE THEORY OF LOGICAL TYPES

MONOGRAPHS IN
MODERN LOGIC SERIES

edited by
G. B. KEENE

THE THEORY
OF LOGICAL TYPES

BY

Irving M. Copi

LONDON

ROUTLEDGE & KEGAN PAUL

THE COLLEGE AND SEMINARY LIBRARY
NAPERVILLE, ILLINOIS

First published 1971
in Great Britain by
Routledge & Kegan Paul Ltd.
Broadway House, 68–74 Carter Lane
London, EC 4V 5EL
Copyright © Irving M. Copi 1971

No part of this book may be reproduced in any form
without permission from the publisher, except for the
quotation of brief passages in criticism

ISBN 0 7100 7026 8

Printed in Great Britain by
Willmer Brothers Limited, Birkenhead

160
c79t

To the memory of Bertrand Russell,
a great philosopher and a great man

120755

CONTENTS

PREFACE

Contemporary writings on logic and philosophy often refer to the Theory of Logical Types. The reader who wants to find out about that theory can consult very different kinds of sources. Some early accounts, like Russell's own, are enormously stimulating but rather loosely written. Some recent formulations are completely rigorous and precise, but do not provide an easily intelligible overview of the theory, the problems it was intended to solve, and the objections that have been raised against it. In this monograph I have tried to give an account of the Theory of Logical Types which shall not be so technical as to repel the non-specialist nor so informal as to disappoint the serious student who wants to see exactly what it is and how it works.

Serious criticisms of type theory are reported here, and where I could do so I have tried to answer them. The Theory of Logical Types raises questions for the philosophy of logic: I have tried to provide a sufficiently trustworthy account of the theory to permit responsible philosophizing about it.

Some of the early work on this monograph was supported by the United States National Science

Foundation. During the winter of 1964–5 parts were presented to Professor Sir Karl Popper's seminar at the London School of Economics and to Professor Stephan Körner's seminar at the University of Bristol. I am grateful for good discussions with those groups. An early draft was read by my colleague Professor John Winnie and I have profited by discussions with him. And it is a pleasure once again to thank my wife for understanding and encouraging the effort that has gone into the present book.

Irving M. Copi

Chapter 1
THE PARADOXES

Around the turn of the century a number of contradictions began to appear within mathematics. The first two of them arose at the outermost reaches of the new mathematics of the infinite. Later ones appeared in the very heart of classical mathematics itself. Some seemed to be more linguistic than mathematical. A subsequent division of these contradictions into two groups, logico-mathematical on the one hand, linguistic or semantic on the other, proved to be an extremely fruitful basis for their classification. Reactions to the contradictions were mixed. At first their importance was minimized; later they were seen to constitute a deadly serious problem. Today contradictions of both sorts are perceived to have led to some of the most exciting and important results in modern logic and mathematics.

1.1 Logical Paradoxes

The first of the modern paradoxes to be published was that of Cesare Burali-Forti in 1897. (A discussion of the early history of this paradox can be found in Copi, 1958.) It concerns the well-ordered class of all ordinal numbers, and its formulation presupposes some familiarity with transfinite ordinal arithmetic. Here we only mention it, and proceed to a detailed account of the Cantor paradox, which is more important for our present purposes.

Scientific studies of the infinite have long been beset with difficulties. In classical antiquity the discovery of incommensurables (such as the side and diagonal of a square) seemed to imply the infinite divisibility of geometrical magnitudes and to destroy the Pythagorean identification of geometry with arithmetic. Zeno's paradoxes of motion, however, such as his 'Achilles and the tortoise', revealed grave and subtle difficulties in the notion of infinite divisibility. Euclid regarded it as axiomatic that the whole is greater than its part, which is surely true of finite quantities. But the Euclidean axiom seems to fail in the case of infinite collections. In 1638 Galileo argued that although squares are only some among numbers, yet 'there are as many squares as there are numbers because they are just as numerous as their roots, and all the numbers are roots' (Galilei, 1946, 31). In 1679 Leibniz observed that since every number can be doubled, the number of even numbers is the same as the number of numbers altogether, and this is a clear case of a whole being no greater than a (proper) part of itself (Leibniz, 1962, I, 338; quoted in Russell, 1903, 306 ff), though Bolzano did not choose to regard it in that light (Bolzano, 1950, 98).

The criterion used by Galileo and Leibniz for deciding that two collections have the same number of members, or are equal in number, is now widely accepted. For a hundred years it has been generally agreed that two classes are equal in number if and only if there is a one-one correspondence between their members. A one-one correspondence is said to obtain between the members of classes *A* and *B* if and only if there is a correlation such that each member of *A* is correlated with one and only one member of *B*, and conversely. For example, in a strictly monogamous community the class of all husbands is equal in number to, or has the same cardinality as, the class of all wives. Without knowing how many husbands or wives there are, we know the classes to be equal in number because marriage provides a one-one correlation of husbands to wives in such communities. Infinite classes as well as finite ones can be shown to be equal in cardinality by exhibiting a one-one correspondence of their members. Thus the class of natural numbers $\{0, 1, 2, \ldots\}$ can be shown to be cardinally equal to the class of all positive rational fractions by enumerating the fractions in the following way. Of two fractions we place first that one the sum of whose numerator and denominator is smaller; and of two fractions whose numerators and denominators add to the same sum, we place first the one whose numerator is smaller. There are only finitely many fractions whose numerators and denominators add to the same sum. We place first that for which the sum is 2, next those for which the sum is 3, then 4, and so on, thus ordering the set of all rational fractions in such a way that to each may be correlated exactly one natural number. Thus we have:

1/1	1/2	2/1	1/3	2/2	3/1	1/4	2/3	3/2	4/1	1/5	...
0	1	2	3	4	5	6	7	8	9	10	...

Any class whose members can be put into one-one correspondence with the natural numbers is said to be *denumerable* (or *enumerable*).

One surprising though inescapable result established by Georg Cantor in the transfinite arithmetic that he founded and developed is that there are different orders of infinity: some infinite classes are demonstrably larger than others (see Cantor, 1915). For example, the class of all real numbers is of higher cardinality than the class of all natural numbers. That it is *non-denumerable* is proved by a method that has come to be called 'the diagonal process'. The diagonal process has been of enormous importance in the development of the paradoxes as well as in other areas of logic and mathematics. To prove that there are more real numbers than there are integers, we consider *any* enumeration of real numbers, i.e. any denumerable list of them. With no loss in generality we confine our attention to real numbers in the interval from 0 to 1, and consider any enumeration of decimal fractions $a_i = \sum_{j=1}^{\infty} (a_{ij} \times 10^{-j})$, where a_{ij} is the j-th digit of the i-th decimal fraction in the following array:

$$\cdot a_{11}\, a_{12}\, a_{13} \ldots a_{1j} \ldots$$
$$\cdot a_{21}\, a_{22}\, a_{23} \ldots a_{2j} \ldots$$
$$\cdot a_{31}\, a_{32}\, a_{33} \ldots a_{3j} \ldots$$
$$\cdots\cdots\cdots\cdots\cdots\cdots$$
$$\cdot a_{i1}\, a_{i2}\, a_{i3} \ldots a_{ij} \ldots$$
$$\cdots\cdots\cdots\cdots\cdots\cdots$$

No such enumeration of real numbers between 0 and 1 can possibly contain all of them, for given any such enumeration there is always a real number between 0 and 1 that is not included in it. Given any such array, a 'missing' real number is specified on its basis by the following diagonal procedure. The missing real number $d = \sum_{k=1}^{\infty} (d_k \times 10^{-k})$ is the decimal fraction $\cdot d_1\, d_2\, d_3\, \ldots\, d_k\, \ldots$ whose k-th digit d_k is specified to be equal to $a_{kk}+3$ if $a_{kk} \leqslant 5$ or equal to $a_{kk}-3$ if $a_{kk} > 5$, where a_{kk} is the k-th digit of the k-th real number in the given array. This diagonal number d is clearly a real number in the interval 0 to 1. And just as clearly it is not in the given array because for any k it differs from the k-th decimal fraction of the array in the k-th decimal place. Therefore no enumeration of real numbers contains all of them, and it is thus proved that the real numbers are non-denumerable.

The proof is a special form of the proof of a more general theorem. The general theorem states that the class of all subclasses of a given class has a higher cardinal number than does the class itself. A simple proof of this general theorem uses a technique quite analogous to the diagonal procedure involved in the special case.

We consider any one-one correlation of all members of a given class with subclasses of that class, and then specify a subclass that is necessarily omitted from any such correlation. This proves that the members of a class cannot be bi-uniquely correlated with the subclasses of that class.

Let M be any class and let all of its members be correlated in a one-one fashion with some or all of its subclasses. There is obviously a one-one correlation between all of its members and *some* of its subclasses, for each member m of M can be correlated bi-uniquely with the unit subclass $\{m\}$ that contains only m itself, from which it follows that the class of all subclasses of M contains at least as many members as M. But now consider any one-one correlation of all members with subclasses. On its basis we can specify a subclass of M that is missing from the correlation. Consider the class W defined to contain all and only those members of M that are not members of the subclasses with which they are correlated. Clearly W is a subclass of M, for only members of M are members of W. But no member of M is correlated with W. For consider any member m of M. It either belongs to W or it does not. If m belongs to W then (by definition of W) m does not belong to the subclass of M with which it is correlated, and belonging to W it is not correlated with W. If m does not belong to W then (again by definition of W) m does belong to the subclass of M with which it is correlated, and not belonging to W it is not correlated with W. So in either case m is not correlated with W. But m was *any* member of M. Therefore *no* member of M is correlated with W, and there is no one-one correlation between members and all subclasses of any given class.

Cantor's proof establishes that there is no greatest class and hence no greatest cardinal number. Given any class M, however large, there is always a still larger class, the class of all subclasses of M. And given any cardinal number α, there is the still larger number 2^{α} (which is the cardinal number of the class of all subclasses of a class whose cardinal number is α).

But there are certain classes which seem to be the largest possible, the number of whose members would seem therefore to be the largest possible number. For example, the class of all entities altogether must be at least as large as the class of all its subclasses, for each of its subclasses, being an entity, is also a member of it. Again, the class of all classes cannot be smaller than the class of all its subclasses, for each of its subclasses, being a class, must be a member of the class itself. And the class of all propositions must be at least as large as the class of all of its subclasses, for to each subclass there corresponds a unique proposition asserting that subclass to be a subclass of the class of all propositions.

Here, now, is the Cantor paradox: There are classes than which none could be larger, and given any class there is one larger than it. This contradiction was known to Cantor himself in 1899, though his versions of it were not published until 1932 (Cantor, 1932, 443, 448). In the forms having to do with the class of all things conceivable, and with the class of all conceivable classes, it was communicated by Cantor to Dedekind in 1899.

Bertrand Russell attempted to apply the reasoning involved in the proof of Cantor's theorem to one of the 'largest possible classes' just referred to (Russell, 1903, 101, 362, 366f.; see also Russell, 1919b, 136). The attempt led him to a new and simpler contradiction

7

that has come to be called the 'Russell Paradox'. Many classes, perhaps most classes, are not members of themselves. Thus the class of all men is not itself a man and so is not a member of the class of all men. But if we consider the class of all classes that are not members of themselves, and ask if *it* is a member of itself, we plunge directly into contradiction. Let W be the class of all classes that are not members of themselves. If W is a member of W then it is a member of the class of all classes that are not members of themselves, so W is not a member of W. But if W is not a member of W then it is not a member of the class of all classes that are not members of themselves, hence it must be a member of itself, that is, W is a member of W. Here is the contradiction made explicit: W is a member of itself if and only if W is not a member of itself. The Russell Paradox is more perspicuous when expressed in symbols. The standard symbolic notation for 'x is a member of M' is '$x \in M$'. From the definition of the class W it follows that for any class x, $x \in W \equiv \sim (x \in x)$. Now substituting '$W$' for the variable '$x$' in the definitionally true equivalence produces the self-contradictory $W \in W \equiv \sim (W \in W)$.

The Russell Paradox was first published in 1903 by Gottlob Frege (Frege, 1903, 253–65; translated in Frege, 1952, 234–44, and in Frege, 1964, 127–43), to whom Russell had communicated it the year before. Russell also published an account of it in 1903 (Russell, 1903, 101–7). It had been discovered independently by Zermelo and communicated to Hilbert before 1903 (Zermelo, 1908b, 118 n; Hilbert, 1926, 169). Another version of the Russell Paradox makes no use of the notion of *class*. Some properties seem to be predicable of themselves, others do not. For example, the property *human* is not predicable of itself. Let us say that any property that is not predicable of itself is *impredicable*. In symbols, Impr $(P) \equiv \sim P(P)$. Is the property *impredicable* impredicable? If it is, then it isn't; but if it isn't, then it is. In symbols, $\text{Impr}(\text{Impr}) \equiv \sim \text{Impr}(\text{Impr})$. This formula follows from the definition of the symbol 'Impr', yet it is self-contradictory (Russell, 1903, 97, 102). Still another version of the Russell Paradox has to do with (binary) relations rather than properties. Let T be the relation that holds between the relations R and S if and only if R does not have the relation R to S. In symbols, $T(R, S) \equiv \sim R(R, S)$. Now substituting '$T$' for both '$R$' and '$S$' in the formula produces the self-contradictory $T(T, T) \equiv \sim T(T, T)$ (*ibid.*, 521. Cf. Russell, 1908, 59f; Whitehead and Russell, 1910, 60). The Russell Paradox of classes can be generalized into infinitely many others of the same general pattern. Instead of defining '$x \in W$' as equivalent to '$\sim (x \in x)$' we could use '$(y) \sim (x \in y \cdot y \in x)$' or '$(y)\,(z) \sim (x \in y \cdot y \in z \cdot z \in x)$', or etc., and the same contradiction can be derived from any of these ϵ-cycles (Quine, 1940, 128). For another generalization *not* involving ϵ-cycles see Quine, 1963, 36.

Another logical paradox is due to Mirimanoff (Mirimanoff, 1917; see also Yuting, 1953; Montague, 1955). It involves the notion of a *grounded* class, defined as any class x for which there is no sequence of (not necessarily distinct) classes $y_1, y_2, y_3, \ldots$ such that $\ldots \in y_3 \in y_2 \in y_1 \in x$. Let W be the class of all grounded classes. If W is grounded then $W \in W$, whence ... $\epsilon\ W\ \epsilon\ W\ \epsilon\ W$, so W is not grounded. But if W is not grounded, then there is a sequence of classes $y_1,\ y_2,\ y_3,\ \ldots$ such that ... $\epsilon\ y_3\ \epsilon\ y_2\ \epsilon\ y_1\ \epsilon\ W$, whence y_1 is not grounded and cannot be a member of W.

The variety of logical paradoxes is truly infinite.

1.2 Semantic Paradoxes

Mathematicians continued to produce new paradoxes. At a mathematical congress in Heidelberg in 1904 two papers were in evident conflict. E. Zermelo presented a proof that any class can be well-ordered, and J. König presented a proof that the continuum (the class of all real numbers) *cannot* be well-ordered.[1] König's paper, published in 1905, involved the notion of *finite definability*. A finite definition must consist of a finite series of letters and punctuation marks. Because there are only finitely many different letters and different punctuation marks altogether, there can be at most a denumerable number of finite definitions. Hence at most a denumerable number of real numbers are finitely definable. But the class of all real numbers was shown by Cantor to be nondenumerable. The nondenumerable class of all real numbers contains a denumerable subclass of real numbers that are finitely definable. That the continuum cannot be well-ordered now follows easily. For if the continuum could be well-ordered, the class of all real numbers *not* capable

[1] A well-ordered class is an ordered class every non-empty subclass of which contains a first element. For a report of the two papers see L. Olivier 1904, 961; 1905, 241.

of finite definition would have a first element. But the first real number not capable of finite definition — — *is* capable of finite definition, for it is finitely definable by means of the phrase just used! This argument was offered by König as a *reductio ad absurdum* proof that the continuum cannot be well-ordered.

This 'result' of König's was discovered independently at about the same time by A. C. Dixon (1906), who went on to remark that 'the least number that cannot be specified without using more than n symbols' leads to a like contradiction for n greater than the number of symbols between the quotation marks in this sentence. In the same year Russell published a new paradox attributed by him to G. G. Berry (Russell, 1906a, 645, note 2). It concerns the fact that 'the least integer not nameable in fewer than nineteen syllables' is itself a name consisting of eighteen syllables. So the least integer not nameable in fewer than nineteen syllables can be named in eighteen syllables — — another contradiction.

The most famous of the present group of contradictions is due to Jules Richard (1905). He observed that because only a denumerable number of real numbers can be finitely defined, the class E of all finitely definable real numbers in the interval between 0 and 1 can be enumerated as a first, a second, a third and so on. If we consider them as infinite decimal fractions, yet another number N in the interval between 0 and 1 can be finitely defined using the Cantor diagonal procedure. N must be a member of E because it is finitely definable and lies between 0 and 1. But N cannot be a member of E, for it differs in its nth digit

11

from the nth member of E, for every n. This is clearly a contradiction. For an interesting variant and application of the Richard paradox, see Carnap, 1937, 213f and 219f; and for a discussion of its implications, see Church, 1934.

Perhaps the most elegant of the present group of paradoxes is that due to Kurt Grelling (Grelling and Nelson, 1907-8). It concerns the fact that some words, such as 'long', 'German' and 'monosyllabic', designate properties that do not belong to the words themselves. Such words will be said to have the property of being *heterological*. Now consider the word 'heterological'. If it is heterological then it has the property it designates and so is not heterological. But if it is not heterological then it does not have the property it designates and so it is heterological. This contradiction is the Grelling paradox.

The earliest known paradox of the present kind is that of the liar. One version of it, called the 'Epimenides', has Epimenides state that all Cretans are liars. But Epimenides was himself a Cretan. Assuming that all *other* Cretan statements are lies, and taking lies in this context to be the same as false statements, there is clearly a contradiction in this statement of Epimenides. If his statement is true, then since it is a Cretan statement it must be false. But if it is false then *some* Cretan statement must be true, and by our assumption that all others are false, Epimenides' own statement must be the true one.

Paradoxes of this kind were known in antiquity and discussed in the Middle Ages. A historical account is to be found in Rüstow (1910; see also Quine, 1966a,

3–23). A more elegant version of the paradox of the liar is due to J. Lukasiewicz (see Grelling, 1936). Consider the following English statement:

> The sentence on page 13, lines 5–6
> of this monograph is not true.

Let us abbreviate the preceding statement by the letter '*S*'. Clearly

> '*S*' is true if and only if *the sentence on page 13, lines 5–6 of this monograph is not true.*

But counting lines and checking the page number verifies that '*S*' is identical with *the sentence on page 13, lines 5–6 of this monograph.* Hence

> '*S*' is true if and only if '*S*' *is not true*

which is an explicit contradiction.

The simplest version of the liar is one proposition, p, asserting that p is false. Here p both implies and is implied by its contradictory, $\sim p$. It is easily generalized along the lines of the ϵ-cycle generalization of the Russell Paradox. If p_1 asserts that p_2 is false and p_2 asserts that p_1 is true, each is equivalent to its own denial. For a discussion of the generalization, see Lewis and Langford (1932, 438–41).

1.3 Classification of the Paradoxes

The paradoxes that have been presented in the preceding two sections under the headings 'logical' and 'semantic' did not arrive with these labels already attached. The earliest modern paradoxes arose in the development of transfinite arithmetic. Not all mathematicians had welcomed the study of the infinite, just as not all mathematicians had welcomed the development of symbolic logic. Henri Poincaré, perhaps the greatest mathematician living at that time, was vigorously opposed to both. A finitist of sorts, Poincaré wrote: *'There is no actual infinite*; the Cantorians have forgotten this, and they have fallen into contradiction' (Poincaré, 1906, 316). And he added: 'The logisticians have forgotten this like the Cantorians, and they have encountered the same difficulties' (*ibid.*, 317). Yet Poincaré had been the first to see a connection between the new paradoxes 'of the infinite' and the ancient puzzle of Epimenides (*ibid.*, 305f). Russell welcomed Poincaré's amalgamation of the liar with the newer paradoxes, reviewed the contradiction of the man who says 'I am lying', and inquired of Poincaré: 'Has this man too forgotten that there is no actual infinite?' (Russell, 1906a, 633).

The first to suggest that there were two fundamentally different kinds of paradoxes was G. Peano, who remarked that Richard's paradox was linguistic rather than mathematical (Peano, 1906, 157). Russell disregarded this suggestion, and provided in his Ramified Type Theory a single resolution for paradoxes of both sorts. The systematic division of these paradoxes into two groups was argued for in detail by F. P. Ramsey in 1926. The logical paradoxes, according to Ramsey, are 'contradictions which, were no provision made against them, would occur in a logical or mathematical system itself. They involve only logical or mathematical terms such as class and number . . .'

14

(Ramsey, 1926, 20). The other contradictions 'are not purely logical, and cannot be stated in logical terms alone; for they all contain some reference to thought, language, or symbolism . . .' (*ibid.*, 20). The notions of definition, designation, truth and falsehood do seem to be essentially involved in paradoxes of the second group. Ramsey called them 'epistemological', but they are usually referred to today as *semantic paradoxes* (Fraenkel and Bar-Hillel, 1958, 9–12; Quine, 1963, 254f).

Both the logical and semantic paradoxes must be distinguished from what have been called 'pseudo-paradoxes'. Perhaps the best known example of a pseudo-paradox is that of the town barber who is supposed to shave all those and only those in the town who do not shave themselves. If he shaves himself then he cannot, but it he does not then he must. Another concerns the crocodile who promises a mother that he will return her child if she can tell him what he is going to do, otherwise he will eat it, and his predicament when the mother tells him that he is going to eat the child. Other examples are easily constructed: the bibliography of all bibliographies that do not include themselves as entries, the inventory list of all inventory lists that do not include themselves as items, etc. All these pseudo-paradoxes are easily resolved simply by drawing the obvious conclusion that there is not, because there cannot be, any such barber or bibliography or inventory list or promise-keeping crocodile who makes such self-defeating promises. This resolution cannot be applied so simply to either the logical or the semantic paradoxes.

But why can't the resolution of the pseudo-paradoxes be applied to the logical or semantical paradoxes? Why can't we simply say that there is no meaningful word such as 'heterological' and no such class as the class of all classes that are not members of themselves, because the assumption that they exist leads to contradiction? The answers to these questions involve the following considerations.

The specification of a non-mathematical, contingent entity generally carries no suggestion that there actually is anything answering to that specification. Characterizations of Greek Gods, perpetual motion machines, barbers with special duties and so on, are not taken to imply that there actually exist any things so characterized. But in sharp contrast, specifications of classes by stating their membership conditions do seem to carry the implication that there are such classes. Quine (1962) put the matter very clearly, writing:

> The almost invariable way of specifying a class is by stating a necessary and sufficient condition for belonging to it. When we have stated such a condition, we feel that we have 'given' the class and can scarcely make sense of there not being such a class. The class may be empty, yes; but how could there not be such a class at all? What substance can be asked for it that the membership condition does not provide?

The Russell Paradox, of course, shows that despite our 'feeling' that stating a membership condition 'gives' a class, not every membership condition does so. What, then, does 'give' a class? Type theory and various kinds of set theory offer alternative, apparently more or less satisfactory answers to this question. But how satisfactory is the suggestion that every membership condition gives a class if its doing so does not imply a contradiction? This suggestion is unacceptable on three counts.

First, to accept this criterion for class existence would entail rejection of the complementation operation of standard elementary Boolean Algebra. The condition $x \in x$ determines the class $\alpha = \{x : x \in x\}$, which does not itself lead to any contradiction. But if we form the complement of α, which Boolean Algebra assures us we can do, we get the Russell class $W = \bar{\alpha} = \{x : \sim(x \in x)\}$ which does lead to contradiction. Hence complementation would no longer be a legitimate operation, and this is surely an unacceptable consequence of the suggestion.

Second, to accept this criterion for class existence would entail that two different classes may each separately be harmlessly given, but not both. For example, $\alpha = \{x : (y) \sim(x \in y)\}$ does not lead to any contradiction, and $\beta = \{x : (y) \sim(y \in x)\}$ does not lead to any contradiction either. But if we consider both as given then their intersection $\alpha \cap \beta = \{x : (y) \sim(x \in y) \cdot (y) \sim(y \in x)\} = \{x : (y)[\sim(x \in y) \cdot \sim(y \in x)]\}$ leads straight to a contradiction (Quine, 1940, 128). In such cases as this, if we wish to preserve class products or intersections, we must regard either α or β as not existing. But how should we choose between them? This is surely an unacceptable consequence of the suggestion.

Third, for quantification theory, as Church (1936)

has shown, there is no decision procedure. That is, no method can be devised which will permit us to decide the truth or falsehood of any given statement involving quantifiers. In particular, therefore, we have no effective way of deciding of an arbitrary given φ whether or not

$$(\exists y)(x \in y \equiv \varphi) \supset p \cdot \sim p.$$

Hence we have no effective way of applying the suggested criterion for class existence. This means that we have no effective way of deciding whether or not a proposed symbol for a class, e.g. $\{x : \varphi\}$, is well-formed or ill-formed. We can live with 'theorem' being a non-effective notion, but we can scarcely accept a notion of 'well-formed formula' or 'significant expression' which is non-effective. It would have to be, however, on the suggestion under consideration, and this is surely an unacceptable consequence of the suggestion.

1.4 Importance of the Paradoxes

It is easy and tempting to deprecate the importance of the paradoxes: to regard them as riddles or jokes that are puzzling and entertaining but without serious implications for logic or mathematics. But they do have the most serious implications.

The emergence of a contradiction shows that a mistake has been made. Now what kind of mistake —or kinds of mistakes—do the paradoxes reveal? At first Russell thought there was an obvious and easily rectified error in the proof of the Burali-Forti paradox, writing that the '...premiss...that the series of all ordinal numbers is well-ordered...must...be rejected...In this way...the contradiction in question can be avoided' (Russell, 1903, 323). And he thought the Cantor paradox showed simply that in Cantor's proof '...that there is no greatest number ...the master has been guilty of a very subtle fallacy' (Russell, 1901, 95; reprinted 1918, 89). Indeed the first paradoxes published arose so close to the frontier of transfinite arithmetic that they occasioned little general distress. But Russell's own paradoxes revealed contradictions in that part of set theory which underlies all other branches of mathematics, and in the notion of predication that is central to logic itself.

Frege acknowledged that Russell's paradox 'shook the foundations' of his carefully worked out logico-mathematical system (Frege, 1903, 253; translated in Frege 1952, 234; and in Frege 1964, 127). The shock of its publication was described vividly by Hilbert, who wrote: '...when it appeared in the mathematical world, it produced literally the effect of a catastrophe' (Hilbert, 1926, 169). Gödel characterized Russell's work on the paradoxes as 'the most important of Russell's investigations', and wrote that: 'By analyzing the paradoxes to which Cantor's set theory had led, he freed them from all mathematical technicalities, thus bringing to light the amazing fact that our logical intuitions (i.e., intuitions concerning such notions as: truth, concept, being, class, etc.) are self-contradictory' (Gödel, 1944, 131).

The paradoxes revealed that the intuitive set theory underlying mathematics required a radical reconstruction if it was to serve as an adequate foundation. The paradoxes revealed that the intuitive logic regarded as the indispensable and sufficient tool for the derivation of mathematical truths also required a radical reconstruction. Looking back, after more than half a century of progress in these areas, we can see that an additional importance of the paradoxes lay in the new investigations and new results that were first provoked by their discovery, and which would scarcely have been attempted had the paradoxes not served to stimulate them. See Fraenkel and Bar-Hillel (1958) for a more extended discussion of the importance of the paradoxes, and Mostowski (1965) for an overview of the more important resultant developments.

Chapter 2
THE SIMPLE THEORY
OF TYPES

The Simple Theory of Logical Types and the Ramified Theory of Logical Types both originated with Bertrand Russell. The first will be discussed in the present chapter, the second in the chapter following. What Russell then called 'The Doctrine of Types' was first published by him in 1903. In Appendix B of his *Principles of Mathematics* Russell wrote: 'The doctrine of types is here put forward tentatively, as affording a possible solution of the contradiction . . .' (Russell, 1903, 523). By 'the contradiction' Russell referred indifferently to both versions of what we have been calling the Russell Paradox. Russell's sponsorship of the theory was highly tentative. Although he remarked earlier in the book that ' . . . the distinction of logical types . . . is the key to the whole mystery' (*ibid.*, 105), he admitted that the early version did not quite work. After pointing out a difficulty, he wrote: 'It seems to follow that the Contradiction requires further subtleties for its solution; but what these are, I am at a loss to imagine' (*ibid.*, 527). Thirty-five years later, in his 'Introduction to the Second Edition' of that book, Russell referred to his formulation in Appendix B as 'only a rough sketch' (Russell, 1938, p. xiii) in which the doctrine of types occurs only 'in a crude form' (*ibid.*, p. viii).

For several years after the publication of the first edition of *Principles of Mathematics*, Russell sought to resolve the paradoxes by other means. But he finally returned to the Doctrine of Types and in 1908 published a version of it which came to be called the Ramified Theory of Logical Types (Russell, 1908; reprinted in Russell, 1956). It was this Ramified Theory that was incorporated in *Principia Mathematica* (Whitehead and Russell, 1910–13). A dozen years later Frank Plumpton Ramsey urged a thoroughgoing revision of the type theory of *Principia Mathematica* (Ramsey, 1926). The proposal had been made earlier by Chwistek (see Chwistek, 1921; Chwistek, 1948, 152–3). Russell later acknowledged that Ramsey's classification of the paradoxes '. . . renders possible a great simplification of the theory of types, which, as it emerges from Ramsey's discussion, ceases wholly to appear unplausible or artificial or a mere *ad hoc* hypothesis designed to avoid the contradictions' (Russell, 1938, p. xiv). Here we have what has come to be known as the Simple Theory of Logical Types. It is very close indeed to Russell's 1903 version.

2.1 Informal Exposition of Simple Type Theory

Russell's earliest explanation of the doctrine of types (Russell, 1903, 523) was the following:

Every propositional function $\varphi(x)$—so it is contended—has, in addition to its range of truth, a range of significance, *i.e.* a range within which x

must lie if $\varphi(x)$ is to be a proposition at all, whether true or false. This is the first point in the theory of types; the second point is that ranges of significance form *types*, *i.e.* if x belongs to the range of significance of $\varphi(x)$, then there is a class of objects, the *type* of x, all of which must also belong to the range of significance of $\varphi(x)$, however φ may be varied . . .

Russell's earliest account of type theory was in terms of individuals and classes. 'A *term* or *individual* is any object which is not a range. This is the lowest type of object' (*ibid.*, 523). . . . 'The next type consists of . . . classes of individuals' (*ibid.*, 524). . . . 'The next type after classes of individuals consists of classes of classes of individuals. Such are, for example, associations of clubs; the members of such associations, the clubs, are themselves classes of individuals' (*ibid.*). Russell had already written that it is

. . . necessary to distinguish (1) terms [individuals], (2) classes [of individuals], (3) classes of classes [of individuals], and so on *ad infinitum*; we shall have to hold that no member of one set [type] is a member of any other set [type], and that $x \in u$ requires that x should be of a set [type] of a degree lower by one than the set [type] to which u belongs. Thus $x \in x$ will become a meaningless proposition; and in this way the contradiction is avoided (*ibid.*, 517).

This account of the Simple Theory of Types is phrased in terms of individuals and classes, and divides into two parts. The first part posits an infinite

c

hierarchy of types: Type 0 consists of all individuals, Type 1 consists of all classes of individuals, and in general Type $m+1$ consists of all classes of entities of Type m. The second part imposes a condition of significance on formulas of the pattern $x \in y$: such a formula is significant if and only if the type of x is one lower than the type of y. It is clear that both parts are required to eliminate the Russell Paradox of the class of all classes that are not members of themselves. It should also be clear that all of the other paradoxes concerning classes are also eliminated. No subclass of a class can be a member of that class, and this suffices to eliminate the Cantor paradox. No class of ordinal numbers can be of the same type as the ordinal numbers that belong to it, and the Burali-Forti paradox is thereby eliminated also. Inspection shows that the Simple Theory of Types suffices to eliminate also the infinitely many paradoxes involving ϵ-cycles. The hierarchy of types together with the rule of significance prevents any definition of a 'grounded' class, and therewith Mirimanoff's paradox vanishes also.

Russell's account of the Simple Theory of Types was more complicated than that just given, because he was concerned also with relations. The admission of relations makes for a much more complicated theory, for one now must posit a new type for relations of individuals, another type for relations of classes of individuals, etc., plus a type for classes of relations of individuals, another type for classes of such classes, etc., plus more types for relations among entities of the types already mentioned, plus more types for classes of such relations, and so on. The Simple Theory of Types is not all that simple. As Russell remarked, '... we obtain an immense hierarchy of types, and it is difficult to be sure how many there may be ...' (*ibid.*, 525). The rule of significance required here is complicated, but it certainly involves the requirement that a sentence asserting a relation among entities is significant if and only if the type of the relation is higher than the types of the *relata*. And this suffices to rule out the paradox of the relation T supposed to hold between the relations R and S if and only if R does not have the relation R to S.

One final paradox remains to be considered: that of the property of being *impredicable*. Here the same (or the same kind of) hierarchy of types is posited: type 0 consists of all individuals, type 1 consists of all properties of individuals, type 2 consists of all properties of properties of individuals, and in general type $n+1$ consists of properties of entities of type n. Again, a condition of significance is imposed on sentences of the pattern $F(x)$: such a sentence is significant if and only if the type of x is one lower than the type of F. It is clear that this apparatus eliminates the version of the Russell Paradox expressed as $\text{Impr}(\text{Impr}) \equiv \sim\text{Impr}(\text{Impr})$. In this formula not only are the expressions flanking the equivalence sign meaningless, but the putative definition of 'Impr(P)' as meaning $\sim P(P)$ collapses also because of the meaninglessness of the expression '$P(P)$'. (This type hierarchy of properties may also be complicated by the presence of various types of relations that may significantly be said to hold among individuals, properties of various types, and relations of various types, as well as properties of such relations and relations of such properties.)

The foregoing sketch of the Simple Theory of Types is not exactly the same as that offered by Russell in 1903. The plausibility of Russell's 1903 version as well as its effectiveness in resolving the paradoxes were diminished by his belief at that time that (1) the sum of any two types is also a type, (2) there is a type containing *all* entities, (3) numbers constitute a type separate and distinct from those in the hierarchies indicated above, (4) predicates are individuals, and (5) '$x \epsilon x$ is sometimes significant, and in these cases its denial is also significant' (*ibid.*, 525–6).

The fundamental doctrine of the Simple Theory of Types, that entities divide into separate categories, some of whose members may not be predicable of others, is an old one, and did not originate from any consideration of the logical paradoxes. Plato discussed analogous category differences, both metaphysical and linguistic, in his dialogue *Sophist*. Aristotle did so more explicitly in Chapter 5 of his *Categories*. Schröder distinguished different logical levels of manifolds or sets in 1890 (Church, 1939), and Frege insisted on different levels of functions and concepts[1].

---

[1] Frege, 1893, 37–40; translated in Frege, 1964, 72–8. Frege's hierarchy of *Stufen* did not prevent the derivation in his system of Russell's Paradox of the class of all non-self-membered classes, but it did suffice to prevent the Russell Paradox of *Impredicable*. See Frege, 1893, 9, n. 3 (Frege, 1964, 38, n. 15) for an important restriction which does permit Frege to avoid the paradox of *Impredicable*—contrary to what is stated in Carnap, 1937, 138.

Husserl proposed categories of meaning in 1913, and later wrote of different 'levels' of 'syntactic forms' and of 'ultimate predicates (predicates that are not predicates of predicates . . .)' (Husserl, 1913; Husserl, 1929; the latter translated in Husserl, 1969).

The informal exposition of Simple Type Theory offered in the present section cannot, of course, be seriously regarded either as a description of any natural language such as English or as a prescription for reforming any natural language. It must be viewed as a recommendation for constructing a special artificial language which shall be free from contradiction at the same time that it is adequate to serve the purposes of mathematical logic. Those purposes can be regarded as two-fold: first, the formulation of a system of logic which shall be adequate for all mathematical reasoning; and second, the formulation of a logical basis in terms of which all mathematical ideas can be defined and from which all mathematical truths can be derived. Those, at any rate, were Russell's and Frege's purposes. We now know that no consistent finitely axiomatizable logical system containing arithmetic can be complete (Gödel, 1931), which means that not all mathematical truths can be derived within any such system. But up to 1931 it was a serious and plausible goal. The more modest goal that has replaced it is the formulation of a consistent language or system of logic in which the bulk of classical mathematics can be established. Such a logical system embodying the Simple Theory of Logical Types is presented in the following section.

2.2 Formalization of the Simple Theory of Types

Perhaps the simplest and most intuitive way to develop a formal system embodying Simple Type Theory is to begin with a first-order functional calculus (also called a 'restricted predicate calculus') and then modify it in the desired direction. The first-order system to be used as our point of departure is the system $\mathscr{F}$ expounded by Geoffrey Keene in an earlier monograph of this series (Keene, 1964). Some parts of $\mathscr{F}$ need not be changed at all. The same five operator symbols '$\sim$', '$\vee$', '$\forall$', '(' and ')' will suffice. We *could* keep the same infinite list of propositional letters 'P', 'Q', 'R', 'S', 'P_1', 'Q_1'), ... (*ibid.*, 31) but we shall not need them and will simply not have them present in the new system under construction. We *could* use the same infinite list of variables 'a', 'b', 'c', 'a_1', 'b_1', ... as our *individual* variables, after supplying each of them with a right-hand superscript '0' to indicate its type. But instead we shall amalgamate them with the infinite list 'F^n', 'G^n', 'H^n', 'F_1^n', 'G_1^n', ... that Keene calls 'predicate letters'. For these symbols in the system $\mathscr{F}$ the superscript n ranged over the positive integers and represented the degree (or adicity) of the predicate: 'F^1' representing a property (of individuals), 'F^2' a binary or dyadic relation (of individuals), 'F^3' a ternary or triadic one, and so on. To allow these symbols to serve in a type theory we must permit the superscripts to range over a quite different collection of elements, which we call *type indices* and define recursively as follows:

(a) 0 is a type index.

(b) If $\tau_1, \tau_2, \ldots, \tau_n$ ($n \geqslant 1$) are type indices then $(\tau_1, \tau_2, \ldots, \tau_n)$ is a type index.

(c) Nothing is a type index unless its being so follows from these rules.

It will be convenient to refer to our individual and predicate letters

$$F^{\tau_i}, G^{\tau_i}, H^{\tau_i}, F_1{}^{\tau_i}, G_1{}^{\tau_i}, \ldots$$

simply as *variables*. Where a variable F has the type index τ as superscript, we shall say that τ *is the type of* F. (The symbols 'τ_i' are not themselves syntactical type designations but are syntactical variables ranging over them. In the object language type indices (type designations) consist exclusively of zeros, parentheses and commas.)

We shall subsequently find it useful to introduce as additional variables the letters 'm' and 'n', with and without numerical subscripts. And we shall also introduce, by means of definitions, a number of constants: '0', '1', '2', $\ldots$; '$\mathrm{I}^{(\tau,\tau)}$', '$=$', '$\mathrm{Sm}^{((\tau),(\tau))}$', and '$\mathrm{N}$', which shall all be regarded as having type indices as superscripts. Later too we shall introduce the functor '$'$' which operating on the numerical symbol 'n' will produce the numerical symbol 'n'' which will be our notation for $n+1$.

Now we can state the formation rules of our new system $\mathscr{F}^{\mathrm{TT}}$ by giving the following recursive definition of well-formed formula (wff):

(i) If the symbols $G_1, G_2, \ldots, G_n$ are of the types, respectively, $\tau_1, \tau_2, \ldots, \tau_n$, then $F(G_1, G_2, \ldots,$

G_n) is a wff if and only if the type of F is $(\tau_1, \tau_2, \ldots, \tau_n)$.

(ii) If A is a wff then $(\sim A)$ is a wff.

(iii) If A and B are wffs then $(A \vee B)$ is a wff.

(iv) If A is a wff and F is a variable then $(\forall F)A$ is a wff.

(v) No formula is a wff unless its being so follows from these rules.

It will be noted that wffs themselves in $\mathscr{F}^{\mathrm{TT}}$ are completely outside the hierarchy of types: no type index attaches to any wff as such. The formulation offered here is in the spirit of Carnap (1937, 84–7; 1958, 81–2). An alternative formulation in which wffs themselves constitute a type can be found in Church (1940).

Illustrative examples come readily to mind. If G_1^0 and G_2^0 are interpreted to denote individuals, and $F^{(0,0)}$ is interpreted to denote the relation that obtains between two individuals when the first is larger than the second, then the wff $F^{(0,0)}(G_1^0, G_2^0)$ will express that G_1^0 is larger than G_2^0. Where $I^{(0,0)}$ denotes identity (of individuals), that G_1^0 is identical with G_2^0 is expressed by the wff $I^{(0,0)}(G_1^0, G_2^0)$. Where $T^{((0,0))}$ is interpreted to denote the transitivity of binary relations of individuals, both the wff $T^{((0,0))}(F^{(0,0)})$ and the wff $T^{((0,0))}(I^{(0,0)})$ express true propositions. If the individual G_1^0 prefers property (of individuals) $H_1^{(0)}$ to property (of individuals) $H_2^{(0)}$, this might be expressed by the wff $P^{(0,(0),(0))}(G_1^0, H_1^{(0)}, H_2^{(0)})$.

Given this symbolism for $\mathscr{F}^{\mathrm{TT}}$, if we adopt the axioms and rules for $\mathscr{F}$ understood as holding for all wffs and variables of $\mathscr{F}^{\mathrm{TT}}$, we obtain an extended predicate calculus embodying the Simple Theory of Types (see Keene, 1964, 33). As in $\mathscr{F}$, so in $\mathscr{F}^{TT}$, we introduce additional useful notations via the following definitions (compare Keene, 1964, 19f, 33):

D1. $(A \to B)$ for $(\sim A \vee B)$
D2. $(A \cdot B)$ for $\sim(\sim A \vee \sim B)$
D3. $(A \leftrightarrow B)$ for $(A \to B) \cdot (B \to A)$
D4. $(F)A$ for $(\forall F)A$
D5. $(\exists F)A$ for $\sim(F)\sim A$.

The Transformation Rules of Inference for $\mathscr{F}^{TT}$ are two in number:

(MP) From A and $A \to B$ to infer B.
(G) From $B \to A$ to infer $B \to (F)A$ provided F is a variable with no free occurrence in B.

Finally, the Axioms of $\mathscr{F}^{TT}$ are the infinity of wffs specified by the following schemata, where A, B, C are wffs and G, F are variables of the same type:

P1. $(A \vee A) \to A$
P2. $A \to (A \vee B)$
P3. $(A \vee B) \to (B \vee A)$
P4. $(A \to B) \to [(C \vee A) \to (C \vee B)]$
P5. $(F) \to \dot{S}_F^G[A]$ provided that no free occurrence of G in A lies within the scope of a quantifier containing F.

The notation $\dot{S}_F^G[A]$ in P5 denotes the result of replacing every free occurrence of F in A by G (*ibid.*, 10f).

The standard definitions for proof and theorem that were given for $\mathscr{F}$ are accepted for $\mathscr{F}^{TT}$ (*ibid.*, 34f).

The Simple Theory of Types

Just as all theorems of a standard Propositional Calculus (interpreted to permit restricted predicate calculus wffs in place of propositional symbols) are theorems in a standard first-order functional calculus such as $\mathscr{F}$, so all theorems of the standard first-order functional calculus $\mathscr{F}$ (interpreted to permit wffs containing variables of all (finite) types in place of wffs of the first-order functional calculus) are theorems of the extended predicate calculus $\mathscr{F}^{TT}$.

In developing a first-order functional calculus metalogically from axiom schemata, every proof established infinitely many theorems of the object language, namely all those wffs of the object language that are denoted by the metalanguage's expression for the theorem(s) being proved. The same holds for the extended predicate calculus embodying Simple Type Theory, $\mathscr{F}^{TT}$, with an *additional* dimension of generality. Every proof for $\mathscr{F}^{TT}$ establishes infinitely many theorems within each of the infinitely many types in which variables may be located. To the extent that our metalogical expressions for wffs of $\mathscr{F}^{TT}$ contain either no type indices for variables or syntactical variables for type indices, to that extent we are taking advantage of the *typical ambiguity* of our expressions, which permits greater ease in expressing wffs and giving proofs.

No paradox can occur in $\mathscr{F}$ because in it no predicate can occupy the position of an argument. But in $\mathscr{F}^{TT}$ a predicate—a variable of any type other than 0—*can* occupy the position of an argument. But if a variable G^{τ} does occupy the position of an argument for a predicate, then that predicate must be of type (τ),

32

which is clearly different from the type τ of its argument G^τ. Hence no predicate can be its own argument, and the Russell Paradox of *Impredicable* cannot be formulated. That the other logical paradoxes are also prevented will become clear as we proceed to develop the system $\mathscr{F}^{\text{TT}}$.

Even with no additional axioms—and three more schemata will be added—it is clear that the system $\mathscr{F}^{\text{TT}}$ is more powerful than the first order predicate calculus $\mathscr{F}$. This is most obvious in connection with *identity*. To incorporate identity theory into a first-order predicate calculus it is necessary to add one or more axioms or axiom schemata to the system[1]. But in our extended predicate calculus $\mathscr{F}^{\text{TT}}$ identity (more precisely, identity for type τ) can be defined as follows:

D6. $I^{(\tau,\tau)}(G_1^\tau, G_2^\tau)$ for $(F^{(\tau)})[F^{(\tau)}(G_1^\tau) \leftrightarrow F^{(\tau)}(G_2^\tau)]$

where $F^{(\tau)}(G_2^\tau)$ is the result of replacing any number of occurrences of G_1^τ in $F^{(\tau)}(G_1^\tau)$ by G_2^τ, provided that no occurrence of G_1^τ replaced is in a well-formed part of $F^{(\tau)}(G_1^\tau)$ of either the form $(G_1^\tau)A$ or $(G_2^\tau)A$.

This definition embodies Leibniz's principle of the identity of indiscernibles (see Church, 1956, fn. 502). From this definition the strong (or total) reflexiveness of $I^{(\tau,\tau)}$ follows immediately, as does also the principle of substitutivity (see Quine, 1966b, 175–82):

$$(F^{(\tau)})(G_1^\tau)(G_2^\tau)\{[I^{(\tau,\tau)}(G_1^\tau, G_2^\tau) \cdot F^{(\tau)}(G_1^\tau)] \to F^{(\tau)}(G_2^\tau)\}.$$

And from these follow the familiar and useful commutativity and transitivity of identity.

[1] Unless the calculus contains only finitely many primitive predicates (see Quine, 1963, 13).

33

The Simple Theory of Types

It will be convenient to introduce the more familiar symbol '=' to express identity, and also to avail ourselves of *typical ambiguity* to avoid the clutter of complicated superscripts. Thus we define

D7. $G_1 = G_2$ for $I^{(\tau,\tau)}(G_1^\tau, G_2^\tau)$.

Here we have an infinite number of definitions, a different one for each different type index that can attach to G_1, with the understanding that G_2 has the same type index as G_1, and that when G_1 and G_2 each has the type index τ, the identity symbol '=' is understood to have the type index (τ,τ). For definiteness, if any context requires it, the type indices for G_1, G_2 and '=' appropriate to that context can easily be written in. This symbolic indefiniteness (ambiguity) which can be made definite (unambiguous) by attaching appropriate type indices, is what is meant by *typical ambiguity*.

The principle of substitutivity already referred to may also be written more simply (availing ourselves of typical ambiguity) as

$$(F)(G_1)(G_2)\{[(G_1 = G_2)\cdot F(G_1)] \to F(G_2)\},$$

where $F(G_2)$ is the result of replacing any number of occurrences of G_1 in $F(G_1)$ by G_2, provided that no occurrence of G_1 replaced is in a well-formed part of $F(G_1)$ of either the form $(G_1)A$ or $(G_2)A$. This principle embodies the essential feature of identity. To say that $G_1 = G_2$ is to say that G_1 and G_2 are interchangeable in any context without altering the truth value of that context, or without loss of truth (*salva veritate*). To speak of interchangeability *salva veritate* reveals clearly that we are speaking of interchangeability of *expressions* in such linguistic contexts as statements, sentences or formulas. The entity named by the expression G_1 is identically the same as the entity named by the expression G_2 if and only if the expressions G_1 and G_2 are interchangeable *salva veritate*.

It is customary to distinguish between the intension and the extension of an expression. The intension of a statement or wff is the meaning or conceptual content or proposition expressed by it, whereas the extension of a propositional symbol or a wff is its truth value. Two propositional symbols or wffs with the same extension are said to be *extensionally equivalent*. The intension of a one-place predicate is a property or attribute, whereas the extension is the class of objects having that property, or to which the attribute may be truly attributed. Two such predicates with the same extension are also said to be *extensionally equivalent*. The intension of a two-place predicate is a binary or dyadic relation, the extension is the class of ordered couples standing in that relation. In general, the intension of a *n*-place predicate is an *n*-adic relation, the extension is a class of ordered *n*-tuples. Two predicates with the same extension are said to be *extensionally equivalent*. We can extend the significance of our symbol for (truth-functional) equivalence to let it stand between predicates, and define this enlarged sense of '$\leftrightarrow$' as follows:

D8. $F_1 \leftrightarrow F_2$ for $(G_1)(G_2) \ldots (G_n)[F_1(G_1, G_2, \ldots, G_n) \leftrightarrow F_2(G_1, G_2, \ldots, G_n)]$

where it is understood that F_1 and F_2 are *n*-place

predicates of the same type and that G_1, G_2, ..., G_n are n distinct variables of appropriate type (or types) to serve as arguments. Extensional equivalence is ordinary (truth-functional) equivalence for propositional symbols and wffs, and is defined for predicates by D8.

It is generally agreed that intension determines extension, but not conversely. Thus two wffs with the same meaning must have the same truth value, but two wffs can have the same truth value but have quite different meanings. Although every property determines a unique class, the class of all things having that property, not every class determines a unique property. Thus several quite different properties might determine exactly the same class, e.g. the property of being a rational animal and the property of being a featherless biped with broad nails each determines the same unique class of all men. But since those properties are different, the class of all men does not determine either of them uniquely.

The term 'extensional' has another, closely related meaning. In a language like the Propositional Calculus (Nidditch, 1962), in which propositional symbols are combined only by means of truth-functional connectives and operators such as '·', '∨', '⊃' (or '→'), '≡' (or '↔'), and '∼' (Faris, 1962), wffs that are equivalent in truth value are obviously interchangeable *salva veritate* (Nidditch, 1962, theorems 38 and 39, 50–9). The familiar truth-functional connectives and operators may be regarded as expressing functions of propositions, and so may the wffs of the Propositional Calculus, which contain propositional symbols as arguments. These functions of propositions are said to be *extensional functions*, and the Propositional Calculus as a language is said to be an *extensional language*. In this sense the term 'extensional' applies to contexts: the general definition of an *extensional context* is a context in which any two symbols that are extensionally equivalent are interchangeable *salva veritate*.

In a first-order functional calculus such as $\mathscr{F}$ predicates as well as propositional symbols occur in wffs. Those wffs of $\mathscr{F}$ which contain only propositional symbols as arguments are the same extensional functions of propositions that occur in the Propositional Calculus. Those wffs of $\mathscr{F}$ which contain predicates (or functions) may be regarded as functions of functions. It is easily proved that in $\mathscr{F}$ extensionally equivalent predicates are interchangeable *salva veritate* (Keene, 1964, 41–4). Hence in $\mathscr{F}$ all functions of propositions and all functions of functions are extensional, and $\mathscr{F}$ itself is an extensional language.

It has generally been agreed that not all functions and not all languages are extensional. Russell was definitely of this opinion in 1908 (reprinted in Russell, 1956, 89), and Whitehead and Russell continued to be of this opinion in the first edition of *Principia Mathematica* (Whitehead and Russell, 1910, 8), writing:

> For example, '*A* believes *p*' is a function of *p* which will vary its truth-value for different arguments having the same truth-value . . . Such functions are not excluded from our consideration, and are included in the scope of any general propositions

we may make about functions; but the particular functions of propositions which we shall have occasion to construct or to consider explicitly are all truth-functions. This fact is closely connected with a characteristic of mathematics, namely, that mathematics is always concerned with extensions rather than intensions.

Going further, the authors of *Principia Mathematica* specified that '... the functions of functions with which we shall be specially concerned will all be extensional functions of functions' (*ibid.*, 22). Thus from the beginning, languages embodying the theory of logical types have been so formulated as to be extensional languages. This was admitted to be a restriction. But it was not a restriction required by type theory. It was rather a restriction imposed for the sake of greater ease in the derivation of mathematics within the language.

Perhaps a few more words may be in order on the topic of extensionality. In 1921 Wittgenstein urged that all propositions are truth functions of elementary propositions, which in his system amounted to the doctrine that all language is extensional (Wittgenstein, 1922, 4.2, 4.4, 5, 5.3, 5.54). Four years later, in the 'Introduction to the Second Edition' of *Principia Mathematica*, Whitehead and Russell came very close to agreeing with this stronger claim, which has come to be called the 'Thesis of Extensionality' (Whitehead and Russell, 1925, p. xiv, 659–66). They wrote:

... another course, recommended by Wittgenstein ... is to assume that functions of propositions are always truth-functions, and that a function can only occur in a proposition through its values. There are difficulties in the way of this view, but perhaps they are not insurmountable. It involves the consequence that all functions of functions are extensional. . . . We are not prepared to assert that this theory is certainly right, but it has seemed worth while to work out its consequences in the following pages.

Carnap later formulated the Thesis of Extensionality 'in a way which is at the same time more complete and less ambitious . . . for every given intensional language S_1, an extensional language S_2 may be constructed such that S_1 can be translated into S_2' (Carnap, 1937, 245, see also 240–60). Regardless of the correctness or incorrectness of the Thesis of Extensionality in either its more or less ambitious form, we insure that our formal system embodying Simple Type Theory $\mathscr{F}^{\mathrm{TT}}$ is an extensional language by adding an infinite number of axioms of extensionality as

P6. $(F_1)(F_2)[(F_1 \leftrightarrow F_2) \to (F_1 = F_2)]$.

Because our language $\mathscr{F}^{\mathrm{TT}}$ is extensional, no distinction is made in it between functions of one argument, properties or classes. Each is what is symbolized by a one-place variable of type other than 0, that is, by a one-place predicate. In what follows, therefore, we can feel free to use the terms 'function (of one argument)', 'property' and 'class' quite interchangeably, regarding these several expressions as synonyms.

39

D

The logistic thesis was first announced by Frege (1884, 99) and independently by Russell (1903, xi, see also Russell, 1919b, 4-10). It is the doctrine that all mathematical terms can be defined by means of strictly logical ones, and that all mathematical truths can be derived from strictly logical truths. This thesis was a fitting climax to the nineteenth century's successful 'arithmetization of analysis', in which the higher branches of mathematics were shown to be reducible to the arithmetic of the natural numbers: 0, 1, 2, 3, ... The logistic thesis then comes down to the doctrine that (the bulk of) the arithmetic of natural numbers can be established in a strictly logical system such as $\mathscr{F}^{TT}$. Arithmetic itself had been systematized by Peano in 1889[1], who formulated an axiom system for arithmetic based on three primitive or undefined terms and five axioms. His first formulation contained four additional axioms dealing with identity, which would today be regarded as part of the underlying logic, and are easily derived in our system $\mathscr{F}^{TT}$. And his first formulation had the natural numbers begin with 1 rather than 0; but subsequent formulations have had them begin with 0.

The three primitive terms in Peano's system are 0, Number and Successor. By 'Number' is meant natural number or non-negative integer. And by 'Successor' is meant the immediate successor, the result of adding 1. The five axioms in Peano's system can be expressed in ordinary English as:

---

[1] The axioms were admittedly borrowed from Dedekind, who had established them on an (informal) logical basis (see Dedekind, 1888, 1890; Wang, 1957).

(1) 0 is a Number.

(2) The Successor of any Number is a Number.

(3) No two Numbers have the same Successor.

(4) 0 is not the Successor of any Number.

(5) Any property that belongs to 0, and also to the Successor of any Number that has that property, belongs to all Numbers.

The last of these axioms is recognizable as the principle of mathematical induction. What must be done to carry through the Frege-Russell program is first, to define Peano's primitive terms using only the symbols available in $\mathscr{F}^{\mathrm{TT}}$, and second, to derive the Peano axioms from the postulates of $\mathscr{F}^{\mathrm{TT}}$. (One more axiom and one more axiom schema must still be introduced for the system $\mathscr{F}^{\mathrm{TT}}$; they will be formulated as they are needed.)

Both Frege and Russell defined numbers as classes. But they differed in what they said natural numbers were classes of. For Russell, a number is defined to be a class of similar classes; whereas for Frege, a number is defined to be a class of *gleichzahlig* (equinumerous, equinumerate, similar) concepts. This difference in their doctrines is not profound: it is a consequence of a peculiarly Fregean distinction between 'objects' and 'concepts': for Frege, classes are objects but concepts (properties or functions) are not objects. In an extensional system like $\mathscr{F}^{\mathrm{TT}}$ in which extensionally equivalent functions are identical, and in which functions are admissible arguments for other functions (of appropriately higher type), the difference between a property and its extension vanishes. In such a system as ours, there is no difference between the Fregean and the Russellean definitions of natural numbers.

It has already been remarked in Chapter 1, 1.1, that two classes are equal in number if and only if there is a one-one correspondence between their members. Any two such classes are said to be *similar*. The same can be said in terms of properties: any two properties are *similar* if and only if there is a one-one correlation between all the things having one property and all the things having the other property. Precisely the same can be said using the language of functions: any two functions are *similar* if and only if there is a one-one correlation between all the things satisfying one function and all the things satisfying the other. We can define similarity within $\mathscr{F}^{TT}$, representing it by the two-place predicate Sm:

D9. $\mathrm{Sm}(F_1, F_2)$ for $(\exists G)\{(H_1)\{F_1(H_1) \to (\exists H_2)[F_2(H_2) \cdot G(H_1, H_2) \cdot (H_3)[(F_2(H_3) \cdot G(H_1, H_3)) \to H_2 = H_3]]\} \cdot (H_1)\{F_2(H_1) \to (\exists H_2)[F_1(H_2) \cdot G(H_2, H_1) \cdot (H_3)[(F_1(H_3) \cdot G(H_3, H_1)) \to H_2 = H_3]]\}\}$

where H_1, H_2, and H_3 are variables of the same type τ, F_1 and F_2 are one-place predicates of type (τ), G is a two-place predicate of type (τ, τ), and Sm is a two-place predicate of type $((\tau), (\tau))$. Since the lowest type index is 0, similarity is defined only for one-place predicates of type (0) or higher. Definition D9 makes use of typical ambiguity to define $\mathrm{Sm}^{((\tau), (\tau))}$ for every type τ. But only one-place predicates of the same type can possibly be similar in the sense here defined.

It is obvious, and can easily be proved for each

type τ, that the binary relation expressed by $Sm^{((\tau),\,(\tau))}$ is reflexive, symmetric and transitive, and is therefore an equivalence relation. Like any other equivalence relation, Sm partitions its field (type) into mutually exclusive classes, all members of any one of which are similar to each other. For any one of these equivalence classes, all of its member classes have the same number. But rather than seek out or posit a property which will belong exclusively to all of the classes in each equivalence class, Frege and Russell took the equivalence class itself as the number, the number of each class belonging to that equivalence class. Thus 2 is the class of all couples and 3 is the class of triples. Alternatively, we can say that 2 is the property that belongs to all couples and to nothing else, and that 3 is the property that belongs to all triples and to nothing else.

To say that a class or property F has the number 0 is to say that the class F has no members, or that the property F belongs to nothing at all. In symbols we have

$$D[0] \quad 0(F) \text{ for } (G) \sim F(G).$$

This definition is typically ambiguous. If G is of the lowest type 0, F must be of type (0), and 0 must be of type ((0)). But where G is of a higher type, say τ, the 0 defined will be of type $((\tau))$. Hence D[0] defines a distinct 0 for each type from ((0)) on up.

To say that a class F has the number 1 is to say that there is some G belonging to it, *and* that for any H, if H belongs to F then $H = G$. In symbols,

$$D[1] \quad 1(F) \text{ for } (\exists G)\{F(G) \cdot (H)[F(H) \rightarrow H = G]\}$$

Here too we have typical ambiguity, with a distinct number 1 defined for each type from $((0))$ on up.

Similarly we may define the numbers 2 and 3:

D[2] $2(F)$ for $(\exists G_1)(\exists G_2)\{F(G_1)\cdot F(G_2)\cdot \sim(G_1 = G_2)\cdot (G_3)[F(G_3) \to (G_3 = G_1 \vee G_3 = G_2)]\}$

D[3] $3(F)$ for $(\exists G_1)(\exists G_2)(\exists G_3)\{F(G_1)\cdot F(G_2)\cdot F(G_3)\cdot \sim(G_1 = G_2)\cdot \sim(G_1 = G_3)\cdot \sim(G_2 = G_3)\cdot (G_4)[F(G_4) \to (G_4 = G_1 \vee G_4 = G_2 \vee G_4 = G_3)]\}$

and so on.

There are three difficulties connected with the indicated sequence of definitions D[0], D[1], D[2], D[3], ... for the natural numbers 0, 1, 2, 3, ... In the first place, the 'and so on' following D[3], or the three dots occurring (twice) in the preceding sentence, are quite clearly not satisfactory. What is required is a more definite prescription for going on from D[n] to D[$n+1$]. The second difficulty is closely connected with the first. One of the primitive terms of the Peano system is 'Number'. It is obvious that we want it to symbolize the set containing all the natural numbers 0, 1, 2, 3, ..., and nothing else. But to define it so in our system $\mathscr{F}^{\text{TT}}$ requires that we have a definite and compendious way of indicating all those natural numbers without pretending that '...' is a legitimate part of the notation of our formal language. (Discussion of the third difficulty will be postponed until we consider Peano's Axiom 3.)

We can rid ourselves of dependence on the inadmissible '...' notation by specifying a definite way, given any natural number n, to define the next natural number n' (this will be our notation for $n+1$). A class F belongs to n' if it is the result of adding exactly one thing to a class G that belongs to n. Of course the thing added must not already belong to G. We can say, then, that class F belongs to n' if and only if there is a class G belonging to n and an H not in G such that F contains H and all members of G and nothing else. This equivalence, readily formulated in $\mathscr{F}^{TT}$, captures the intended meaning of Peano's primitive term 'Successor'. Formally, we define n' to be the successor of n as follows:

$$\mathbf{D}[n'] \ \ n'(F) \text{ for } (\exists G)\{n(G)\cdot(\exists H)\{\sim G(H)\cdot(H_1)[F(H_1) \\ \leftrightarrow (G(H_1) \vee H_1 = H)]\}\}$$

We already have captured the intended meaning of Peano's primitive term '0' with our definition D[0], for which an alternative, equally acceptable, equivalent formulation can be given as

$$\mathrm{D}[0] \ \ 0(F) \text{ for } F(G) \leftrightarrow \sim (G = G).$$

To give a formal definition of Peano's primitive term 'N' it will be useful to remark that the *general* definition of a cardinal number as the class of all classes similar to each other is too broad to capture the intended sense of 'N'. There are infinite cardinal numbers as well as finite ones, and we want 'N' to name the class of finite cardinal numbers only. There are alternative, equally satisfactory ways of distinguishing finite from infinite cardinal numbers (see Cantor, 1915). We shall adopt as our criterion for finite cardinal number or natural number the property of possessing every attribute of 0 that is hereditary under the operation of adding 1. Obviously 0 is a natural number in this sense, and so is 1 because 1 results from 0 by the operation of adding 1, and so does 2, and so on. And these are the only ones that have all hereditary attributes of 0. Formally, then, we can define the set of all natural numbers as follows:

$$D[N]\ N(G)\ \text{for}\ (F)\{[F(0)\cdot(m)[F(m) \to F(m')]] \to F(G)\}$$

Having defined the Peano primitives within $\mathscr{F}^{\text{TT}}$, we turn next to deriving the five Peano Axioms as theorems of $\mathscr{F}^{\text{TT}}$. Another axiom schema for $\mathscr{F}^{\text{TT}}$ itself is required for the derivation of Peano's Axiom 3, but the other four are easily established within the part of $\mathscr{F}^{\text{TT}}$ already presented. All steps in the proofs, except those which make reference to the definitions already presented, proceed in accordance with rules and theorems that parallel those of $\mathscr{F}$.

Peano's Axiom 1. $\vdash N(0)$

Proof: $\vdash [F(0)\cdot(m)[F(m) \to F(m')]] \to F(0)$
$\vdash (F)\{[F(0)\cdot(m)[F(m) \to F(m')]] \to F(0)\}$
$\vdash N(0)$ by $D[N]$

Peano's Axiom 2. $\vdash (n)[N(n) \to N(n')]$

Proof: Here (and for Axiom 5 below) we derive the desired result from two assumptions and then use the Deduction Theorem to complete the proof. Our two premisses here are:
$N(n),\ F(0)\cdot(m)[F(m) \to F(m')]$

$\vdash N(n)$ premiss
$\vdash (F)\{[F(0)\cdot(m)[F(m) \to F(m')]] \to F(n)\}$ by $D[N]$
$\vdash [F(0)\cdot(m)[F(m) \to F(m')]] \to F(n)$

$\vdash F(0) \cdot (m)[F(m) \to F(m')]$ premiss

$\vdash F(n)$

$\vdash (m)[F(m) \to F(m')]$

$\vdash F(n) \to F(n')$

$\vdash F(n')$

$N(n) \vdash [F(0) \cdot (m)[F(m) \to F(m')]] \to F(n')$

$\vdash (F)\{[F(0) \cdot (m)[F(m) \to F(m')]] \to F(n')\}$

$\vdash N(n')$ by $\mathbf{D}[N]$

$\vdash N(n) \to N(n')$

$\vdash (n)[N(n) \to N(n')]$

Peano's Axiom 4. $\vdash (n)[N(n) \to \sim (0 = n')]$

Proof: Let $F(G)$ be $\sim H_1(G) \cdot H_1(G)$ or, alternatively, $\sim (G = G)$.

(1) $\vdash \sim F(G)$

      $\vdash G = G$

      $\vdash G = G \vee H(G)$

      $\vdash [G = G \vee H(G)] \cdot \sim F(G)$

      $\vdash \sim \{[G = G \vee H(G)] \to F(G)\}$

      $\vdash \sim \{F(G) \leftrightarrow [H(G) \vee G = G]\}$

      $\vdash (\exists G_1) \sim \{F(G_1) \leftrightarrow [H(G_1) \vee G_1 = G]\}$

      $\vdash \sim (G_1)\{F(G_1) \leftrightarrow [H(G_1) \vee G_1 = G]\}$

      $\vdash \sim \{\sim H(G) \cdot (G_1)\{F(G_1) \leftrightarrow [H(G_1) \vee G_1 = G]\}\}$

      $\vdash (G) \sim \{\sim H(G) \cdot (G_1)\{F(G_1) \leftrightarrow [H(G_1) \vee G_1 = G]\}\}$

      $\vdash \sim (\exists G)\{\sim H(G) \cdot (G_1)\{F(G_1) \leftrightarrow [H(G_1) \vee G_1 = G]\}\}$

      $\vdash \sim \{n(H) \cdot (\exists G)\{\sim H(G) \cdot (G_1)\{F(G_1) \leftrightarrow [H(G_1) \vee G_1 = G]\}\}\}$

      $\vdash (H) \sim \{n(H) \cdot (\exists G)\{\sim H(G) \cdot (G_1)\{F(G_1) \leftrightarrow [H(G_1) \vee G_1 = G]\}\}\}$

      $\vdash \sim (\exists H)\{n(H) \cdot (\exists G)\{\sim H(G) \cdot (G_1)\{F(G_1) \leftrightarrow [H(G_1) \vee G_1 = G]\}\}\}$

$$\vdash \sim n'(F) \qquad \text{by D}[n']$$
$$\vdash (G) \sim F(G) \qquad \text{from (1)}$$
$$\vdash 0(F) \qquad \text{by D}[0]$$
$$\vdash \sim (0 = n') \qquad \text{by D7}$$
$$\vdash N(n) \to \sim (0 = n')$$
$$\vdash (n)[N(n) \to \sim (0 = n')]$$

Peano's Axiom 5. $\vdash (F)\{\{F(0) \cdot (n)\{N(n) \to [F(n) \to F(n')]\}\} \to (n)[N(n) \to F(n)]\}$

Proof:

$F(0) \cdot (n)\{N(n) \to [F(n) \to F(n')]\}, \; N(n)$

1.	$\vdash N(n)$	premiss
2.	$\vdash (n)\{N(n) \to [F(n) \to F(n')]\}$	premiss
3.	$\vdash N(n) \to [F(n) \to F(n')]$	
4.	$\vdash F(n) \to F(n')$	
5.	$\vdash (F)\{[F(0) \cdot (m)[F(m) \to F(m')]] \to F(n)\}$	
		1, D[N]
6.	$\vdash [F(0) \cdot (m)[F(m) \to F(m')]] \to F(n)$	
7.	$\vdash F(0)$	premiss
8.	$\vdash (m)[F(m) \to F(m')]$	from 4
9.	$\vdash F(0) \cdot (m)[F(m) \to F(m')]$	from 7, 8
10.	$\vdash F(n)$	from 6, 9

$F(0) \cdot (n)\{N(n) \to [F(n) \to F(n')]\} \; \vdash N(n) \to F(n)$

$F(0) \cdot (n)\{N(n) \to [F(n) \to F(n')]\} \; \vdash (n)[N(n) \to F(n)]$

$\vdash \{F(0) \cdot (n)\{N(n) \to [F(n) \to F(n')]\}\} \to (n)[N(n) \to F(n)]$

$\vdash (F)\{\{F(0) \cdot (n)\{N(n) \to [F(n) \to F(n')]\}\} \to (n)[N(n) \to F(n)]\}$

Peano's Axiom 3, which we formulate as

$$(m)(n)\{[N(m) \cdot N(n) \cdot \sim (m = n)] \to \sim (m' = n')\},$$

differs from his other Axioms in involving certain

48

existence assumptions. It will be useful to focus on natural numbers of the lowest type, which is ((0)). (It is easily verified that the difficulty to be discussed holds also for natural numbers of every higher type in $\mathscr{F}^{\text{TT}}$.) That two numbers (of this lowest type) cannot have the same successor is readily proved in case neither of the numbers is the total number of individuals. But if n is the total number of individuals in the entire universe, that is, if $n(G) \leftrightarrow (H)[G(H) \leftrightarrow H = H]$, or, to put it in a different but strictly equivalent way, if $n(G) \leftrightarrow (H)G(H)$, then the number n' turns out to have no members at all, and is the null or empty class of type ((0)). For by our definition $D[n']$,

$$n'(F) \leftrightarrow (\exists G)\{n(G) \cdot (\exists H)\{\sim G(H) \cdot (H_1)[F(H_1) \leftrightarrow (G(H_1) \vee H_1 = H)]\}\}$$

whence it follows from $n'(F)$ that $(\exists G)[n(G) \cdot (\exists H) \sim G(H)]$, which is impossible on our assumption that *all* individuals belong to G if $n(G)$ and n is the total number of individuals in the universe. Hence $\sim(\exists F)n'(F)$, and n' is the empty class. But then n'', the successor of n', is the empty class also. For by definition $D[n']$,

$$n''(F) \leftrightarrow (\exists G)\{n'(G) \cdot (\exists H)\{\sim G(H) \cdot (H_1)[F(H_1) \leftrightarrow (G(H_1) \vee H_1 = H)]\}\}$$

whence it would follow from $n''(F)$ that $(\exists G)n'(G)$, which we have seen to be false. Hence $\sim(\exists F)n''(F)$, and n'' is the empty class. And since there is only one empty class of type ((0)) by our axiom of extensionality P6, it follows that $n' = n''$. But $N(n)$ and

$N(n')$ and $\sim(n = n')$. Hence we have $[N(n)\cdot N(n')\cdot \sim (n = n')\cdot(n' = n'')]$, which proves that Peano's Axiom 3 is false if there are only finitely many individuals. So if we want to derive *all* of Peano's Axioms as theorems in $\mathscr{F}^{\mathrm{TT}}$ we shall have to strengthen our system by adding to it an axiom of infinity.

Perhaps it should be pointed out, in passing, that the empty set $\Lambda^{((0))}$ of type $((0))$ is entirely different from the natural number zero of that type, $0^{((0))}$. The empty set $\Lambda^{((0))}$, which can be defined either by $\Lambda^{((0))}(F^{(0)})\leftrightarrow\sim(F^{(0)} = F^{(0)})$ or by $\sim(\exists F^{(0)})\Lambda^{((0))}(F^{(0)})$, has no members at all, whereas $0^{((0))}$ does have a member, exactly one, which is the empty set of the next lower type, $\Lambda^{(0)}$. In short, $0^{((0))}(\Lambda^{(0)})$ but $\sim\Lambda^{((0))}(\Lambda^{(0)})$, whence $\sim(0^{((0))} = \Lambda^{((0))})$.

Various different formulations have been suggested for the needed axiom of infinity. The one used in *Principia Mathematica* (II, 203,*120.03) will be adopted for $\mathscr{F}^{\mathrm{TT}}$ as

P7. $(F^{((0))})[N^{(((0)))}(F^{((0))}) \rightarrow (\exists G^{(0)})F^{((0))}(G^{(0)})]$.

This is a single axiom rather than an axiom schema. No typical ambiguity occurs here, nor is any needed, because if type 0 contains infinitely many individuals, type (0) will contain infinitely many classes of individuals, and so on. Hence the full array of natural numbers 0, 1, 2, 3, ... exist as distinct classes in every type from $((0))$ on up.

There have been many attempts to prove, rather than to postulate, the existence of infinite classes. Several such putative proofs were accepted as valid by Russell in 1903 (Russell 1903, 357–8), but were rejected by him in *Principia Mathematica* (Whitehead and Russell, 1910, II, 183). Those arguments, and others were subjected to careful analysis and shown to be fallacious in 1919 (Russell, 1919b, 137–41). The most plausible attempt to prove the existence of infinitely many natural numbers, by defining $n+1$ as '... the Number which belongs to the concept "member of the series of natural numbers ending with n" ...' (Frege, 1884, 94), was criticized by Russell in the following words (Russell, 1919b, 138):

> The argument that the number of numbers from 0 to n (both inclusive) is $n+1$ depends upon the assumption that up to and including n no number is equal to its successor, which, as we have seen, will not always be true if the axiom of infinity is false.

Zermelo's set theory (Zermelo, 1908b, Axiom VII) contains an explicitly assumed axiom of infinity, although he was able to specify the infinitely many members of the infinite set postulated. These were the empty set, Λ, the set containing that set as its only member, $\{\Lambda\}$, the set containing *that* set as its only member, $\{\{\Lambda\}\}$, and so on. Zermelo had no problem with the existence of these infinitely many elements: Λ, $\{\Lambda\}$, $\{\{\Lambda\}\}$, $\{\{\{\Lambda\}\}\}$, ..., but needed a special axiom of infinity to make sure that they could all be aggregated into a single collection, because his set theory required an explicit axiom or rule for constructing each new (kind of) set out of sets already given or constructed. All of these sets Λ, $\{\Lambda\}$, $\{\{\Lambda\}\}$.... exist for $\mathscr{F}^{\mathrm{TT}}$, but they are all of different logical types: the first of type (0), the second of type ((0)), the third of type (((0))), and so on. And being of different logical types, no two of them can satisfy the same function, have the same property, or belong to the same class. So Zermelo's infinite set is ruled out by the Simple Theory of Types. For any system embodying Simple Type Theory an axiom of infinity is required for the lowest type, and then even (and ever) larger infinite classes are available as higher types are considered.

The actual derivation of Peano's Axiom 3 in $\mathscr{F}^{\mathrm{TT}}$ is not difficult, but is too lengthy to be reproduced here.

One final axiom schema is required for $\mathscr{F}^{\mathrm{TT}}$ to be adequate for arithmetic operations on numbers, both finite and infinite. It is easy enough to define addition and multiplication for natural numbers by the following recursive definitions of $+$ and $\times$:

$$\text{addition} \quad \begin{cases} m+0 = m \\ m+n' = (m+n)' \end{cases}$$

$$\text{multiplication} \begin{cases} m\times 0 = 0 \\ m\times n' = (m\times n)+m. \end{cases}$$

But from Russell's point of view (Russell, 1919b, 117),

> In defining the arithmetical operations, the only correct procedure is to construct an actual class ... having the required number of terms. This sometimes demands a certain amount of ingenuity, but it is essential in order to prove the existence of the number defined.

In any event, there are obvious advantages to

defining arithmetic operations in such a way that they will be applicable in the case of infinite as well as finite numbers. Thus to multiply m by n we need a class F containing m terms and a class G containing n terms. If we now consider the class of all ordered couples whose first element is from F and whose second element is from G, which is called the 'Cartesian Product' of F and G, the product $m \times n$ is the number of this class of ordered couples. Each ordered couple gives us a selection of one element from F and one element from G. We may regard each element of the Cartesian Product of F and G as produced by a selection or choosing of one element from each of the classes F and G. Now if we wish to multiply together n_1, n_2, n_3, ..., which are the numbers of elements in the classes F_1, F_2, F_3, ..., the arithmetic product will be the number of terms in the Cartesian Product $F_1 \times F_2 \times F_3 \times$ ... Where there are only finitely many classes F_1, F_2, F_3, ..., and each of them contains only finitely many members, with a little ingenuity the Cartesian Product can be constructed. But where the number of classes is infinite, the situation is otherwise. A separate axiom is required to guarantee the existence of a class which will contain exactly one member from each of the classes F_1, F_2, F_3, ... whose cardinal numbers are to be multiplied. Because of its connection with the multiplication of cardinal numbers, such an axiom is sometimes called the 'multiplicative principle'. But because it specifies a class which in effect is produced by choosing one element from each of a set of classes, the axiom is more often called the 'axiom of choice'. There are

53

other propositions to which the axiom is logically equivalent, for example, that any two cardinal numbers are either equal or one is larger than the other, or the proposition that any class can be well-ordered (Lemmon, 1968, 111–20).

There are alternative formulations of the axiom of choice. A fairly standard formulation has it say that for any set F of disjoint classes G_1, G_2, ..., there is a set G_c such that for any nonempty class G in F there is exactly one element H_c that belongs to both G and G_c. Here G_c is the selection set for F (compare Carnap, 1937, 92, PS II 21). In symbols, we have:

P8. $(G_1^{(\tau)})(G_2^{(\tau)})\{[F^{((\tau))}(G_1^{(\tau)}) \cdot F^{((\tau))}(G_2^{(\tau)})] \rightarrow (H_1^{\tau})[[G_1^{(\tau)}$
$(H_1^{\tau}) \cdot G_2^{(\tau)}(H_1^{\tau})] \rightarrow G_1^{(\tau)} = G_2^{(\tau)}]\} \rightarrow (\exists G_c^{(\tau)})\{(G^{(\tau)})$
$[F^{((\tau))}(G^{(\tau)}) \rightarrow [(\exists H_2^{\tau})G^{(\tau)}(H_2^{\tau}) \rightarrow (\exists H_c^{\tau})(H_3^{\tau})[[G^{(\tau)}$
$(H_3^{\tau}) \cdot G_c^{(\tau)}(H_3^{\tau})] \leftrightarrow H_c^{\tau} = H_3^{\tau}]]]\}$

Here P8 is an axiom schema, providing for the existence of a selection set for every set of classes of each type. The Simple Theory of Types does not intrinsically involve axiom P7 or axiom schemas P6 and P8; they are required, however, if the system $\mathscr{F}^{TT}$ is to serve as an adequate basis for mathematics.

2.3 An Alternative Formulation of Simple Type Theory

A much more graceful system of Simple Type Theory is made possible by the Wiener-Kuratowski reduction of relations-in-extension to classes of classes (Wiener, 1912; Kuratowski, 1920). We can avoid thereby such complicated type indices as those used in developing $\mathscr{F}^{TT}$ in the preceding section. The underlying predicate calculus itself is simplified by taking the two-place predicate 'ϵ' as the only primitive term in addition to variables, quantifiers, and truth-functional connectives. In the system to be sketched here, which we shall call 'STT', we begin with just four operator symbols '$\sim$', '$\vee$', '(', ')', the special symbol 'ϵ', and an infinite set of variables

$$m^n, \ n^n, \ u^n, \ v^n, \ w^n, \ x^n, \ y^n, \ z^n, \ m_1^n, \ n_1^n, \ u_1^n, \ldots$$

whose superscripts are 0, 1, 2, 3, ..., which are the only type indices needed. The type 0 is that of individuals, and the type $n+1$ is that of classes of elements of type n. The symbol 'n' itself is metalogical: the only superscripts on our variables are the arabic numerals '0', '1', '2', '3', ...

The recursive definition of wff in STT is somewhat simpler:

(i) $x^m \, \epsilon \, y^n$ is a wff if and only if $m+1 = n$.
(ii) If A is a wff then $(\sim A)$ is a wff.
(iii) If A and B are wffs than $(A \vee B)$ is a wff.
(iv) If A is a wff and x is a variable then $(x)A$ is a wff.
(v) No formula is a wff unless its being so follows from these rules.

Much the same definitions are used here that were used in $\mathscr{F}^{TT}$:

D1. $(A \rightarrow B)$ for $(\sim A \vee B)$
D2. $(A \cdot B)$ for $\sim(\sim A \vee \sim B)$
D3. $(A \leftrightarrow B)$ for $(A \rightarrow B) \cdot (B \rightarrow A)$
D4. $(\exists x)A$ for $\sim(x)\sim A$

The same initial five axioms and rules are adopted

55

E

for STT that were presented for $\mathscr{F}^{TT}$, adapted, of course, to the new notation.

It is convenient to introduce a notation for *class abstraction* into STT. We do so by means of the following pair of definitions, where it is understood that 'Fx^n' is our metalogical reference to any wff containing at least one occurrence of the variable 'x^n'.

D5. $y^n \epsilon \{x^n: Fx^n\}$ for $(\exists z^{n+1})(x^n)\{[x^n \epsilon z^{n+1} \leftrightarrow$
$$Fx^n] \cdot y^n \epsilon z^{n+1}\}$$

D6. $\{x^n: Fx^n\} \epsilon y^{n+2}$ for $(\exists z^{n+1})(x^n)\{[x^n \epsilon z^{n+1} \leftrightarrow$
$$Fx^n] \cdot z^{n+1} \epsilon y^{n+2}\}$$

The notation '$\{x^n: Fx^n\}$' we shall call, following Quine (1963), an *abstract*. The abstract '$\{x^n: Fx^n\}$' symbolizes the class of objects x^n satisfying the condition Fx^n. Definitions from here on are to be understood as holding both for variables and with abstracts in place of free variables.

We express our definition of identity (for variables of type n) as:

D[=] $x^n = y^n$ for $(z^{n+1})(x^n \epsilon z^{n+1} \leftrightarrow y^n \epsilon z^{n+1})$

and our axiom of extensionality as

P6. $(z)(z \epsilon x \leftrightarrow z \epsilon y) \rightarrow x = y$.

The familiar notions '$\{x\}$', '$\{x, y\}$', '$\{x, y, z\}$', ... are defined as abbreviating '$\{u: u = x\}$', '$\{u: u = x \vee u = y\}$', '$\{u: u = x \vee u = y \vee u = z\}$', ..., respectively.

The abstraction notation permits an easy explanation of the Wiener-Kuratowski reduction of relations-in-extension to classes. We remarked in the preceding section that the extension of a two-place predicate is a class of ordered couples. The usual notation for the ordered couple whose first element is x and whose second element is y is '$\langle x, y \rangle$'. The ordered pair $\langle x, y \rangle$ must be distinguished from the class $\{x, y\}$ containing the two elements of the ordered pair. The ordered pairs $\langle x, y \rangle$ and $\langle y, x \rangle$ are distinct, whereas $\{x, y\} = \{y, x\}$. The identity conditions for ordered pairs $\langle x, y \rangle$ and $\langle z, w \rangle$ are easy to specify: $\langle x, y \rangle = \langle z, w \rangle$ if and only if $x = z$ and $y = w$. We define the ordered pair as a class, but not simply as the class containing the two elements of the ordered pair. Instead we define it as follows:

$$\mathbf{D} \langle \, \rangle : \quad \langle x, y \rangle \text{ for } \{\{x\}, \{x, y\}\}.$$

Thus $\langle x, y \rangle$ is the class whose two members are classes, one of which contains only the first element of the ordered pair, the other of which contains both elements of the ordered pair. Thus the order can be 'recaptured' from the abstract by our defining convention that the first element of the ordered pair is the element which belongs to both classes contained in the class $\{\{x\}, \{x, y\}\}$. The ordered pair $\langle y, x \rangle$ is $\{\{y\}, \{y, x\}\}$, clearly different from $\{\{x\}, \{x, y\}\}$, which is the ordered pair $\langle x, y \rangle$. The ordered n-tuple $\langle x_1, x_2, \ldots, x_n \rangle$, were it needed, could be defined analogously as $\{\{x_1\}, \{x_1, x_2\}, \ldots, \{x_1, x_2, \ldots, x_n\}\}$.

The usual class operations of ordinary Boolean Algebra are easily defined as follows:

$\mathbf{D} \cup : \quad x \cup y \text{ for } \{z : z \in x \vee z \in y\}$
$\mathbf{D} \cap : \quad x \cap y \text{ for } \{z : z \in x \cdot z \in y\}$
$\mathbf{D}\bar{x} : \quad \bar{x} \quad \text{ for } \{z : \sim(z \in x)\}$

The Simple Theory of Types

And the empty classes for types $n = 1, 2, 3, \ldots$ are defined by:

DΛ: Λ^n for $\{x^{n-1}: \sim(x^{n-1} = x^{n-1})\}$.

These in turn permit simpler definitions of Peano's primitive terms:

D[0] 0   for $\{\Lambda\}$
D[n'] n' for $\{x: (\exists y)[y \in x \cdot x \cap \{y\} \in n]\}$
D[N] N for $\{x: (y)[[0 \in y \cdot (m)(m \in y \to$
$$m' \in y)] \to x \in y]\}$$

The axiom of infinity is formulated in STT as:

P7. $(n)[(n \in N) \to (\exists x)(x \in n)]$

The axiom of choice asserts that for any set z of disjoint classes there is a selection set w containing exactly one member of each class belonging to z:

P8. $(x)(y)[(x \in z \cdot y \in z) \to x \cap y = \Lambda] \to$
$(\exists w)(u)\{[u \in z \cdot \sim(u = \Lambda)] \to (w \cap u \in 1)\}$.

In $\mathscr{F}^{\text{TT}}$ the existence of a property F belonging to all and only those objects x satisfying a condition $(\ldots x \ldots)$ was provable if that condition could be formulated in the language. For by the typically ambiguous rules and axioms carried over into $\mathscr{F}^{\text{TT}}$ from $\mathscr{F}$ we have:

(1) $\vdash (x)[G(x) \leftrightarrow G(x)]$
(2) $\vdash (\exists F)(x)[F(x) \leftrightarrow G(x)]$
(3) $\vdash (G)(\exists F)(x)[F(x) \leftrightarrow G(x)]$
(4) $\vdash (\exists F)(x)[F(x) \leftrightarrow (\ldots x \ldots)]$

Any open sentence $(\ldots x \ldots)$ can be introduced into

(4) from (3) by P5. And by the axiom of extensionality, we have thereby proved the existence of a *class* of objects satisfying any condition that can be formulated in the language. This does not reintroduce the paradoxes of course, because any formula involving ϵ-cycles is not a wff of either $\mathscr{F}^{\mathrm{TT}}$ or STT. It does show, however, what strong existence assumptions for classes are implicit in the notations of $\mathscr{F}^{\mathrm{TT}}$. The notation of STT does not contain these implicit existence assumptions, so they must be assumed explicitly as an additional axiom schema of comprehension (Quine, 1963, 260), which we formulate as:

P9. $(\exists y^{n+1})(x^n)[(x^n \, \epsilon \, y^{n+1}) \leftrightarrow Fx^n]$.

The system STT, patterned after Quine's 1963 formulation, '. . . is what one tends to think of today as Russell's theory of types. It seems to have been presented in this form first by Tarski and Gödel' (*ibid.*, 261; compare Tarski, 1956, 110, 113f; and Gödel, 1931).

It must not be thought that STT and $\mathscr{F}^{\mathrm{TT}}$ are *exactly* equivalent formulations of the same theory. For both of them there are no classes of mixed types: in STT we have $(\exists z)(x^m \, \epsilon \, z \cdot y^n \, \epsilon \, z)$ entailing $m = n$; and in $\mathscr{F}^{\mathrm{TT}}$ we have $(\exists F)[F(G^{\tau_i}) \cdot F(H^{\tau_j})]$ entailing $\tau_i = \tau_j$. It follows, then, that in STT the Wiener-Kuratowski reduction of binary relations to sets of ordered pairs imposes the restriction that we admit only relations that are homogeneous, i.e. which relate only terms of the same type.

What happens, then, to heterogeneous relations in STT? There are none, but we have something which can serve as an acceptable substitute. If we want to consider a relation between x^n and y^{n+1} we can consider instead the corresponding relation between $\{x^n\}$ and y^{n+1}, which will be a legitimate set of ordered pairs $\langle\{x^n\}, y^{n+1}\rangle$ defined as $\{\{\{x^n\}\}, \{\{x^n\}, y^{n+1}\}\}$. More generally, to deal with a relation between x^m and y^n ($m \neq n$) we deal instead with either $\langle\{\{\ldots \{x^m\}\ldots\}\}, y^n\rangle$ where the number of pairs of braces surrounding x^m is $n-m$, or with $\langle x^m, \{\{\ldots \{y^n\}\ldots\}\}\rangle$ where the number of pairs of braces surrounding y^n is $m-n$.

But this shows that STT is weaker than $\mathscr{F}^{TT}$, because in $\mathscr{F}^{TT}$ there is a difference between $F^{((\tau),((\tau)))}(G^\tau, H^{(\tau)})$ and $F^{(((\tau)),((\tau)))}(G^{(\tau)}, H^{(\tau)})$ even where $(G_1^\tau)[G^{(\tau)}(G_1^\tau) \leftrightarrow (G_1^\tau = G^\tau)]$, which asserts that $G^{(\tau)}$ is the unit class whose only member is G^τ. Hence in $\mathscr{F}^{TT}$ there is a clear distinction which is obliterated in STT. It is not claimed that more *needed* or *important* results are obtained in $\mathscr{F}^{TT}$ than in STT. It is merely remarked that there is this difference, and that the two formulations are not *strictly* equivalent.

2.4 Criticisms of the Simple Theory of Types

A considerable variety of objections to type theory have been raised since the theory was first suggested in 1903. Some of these objections are more specifically directed against the Ramified Theory, and will be considered in the following chapter. Here we shall examine three that are directed against the Simple Theory of Types, and shall indicate possible replies that may be made in defense of the Theory.

The Simple Theory of Types

Objection 1 The first objection to the Simple Theory of Types has been stated most forcefully by Quine (1953, 91f.):

> But the theory of types has unnatural and inconvenient consequences. Because the theory allows a class to have members only of uniform type, the universal class V gives way to an infinite series of quasi-universal classes, one for each type. The negation $-x$ ceases to comprise all nonmembers of x, and comes to comprise only those nonmembers of x which are next lower in type than x. Even the null class Λ gives way to an infinite series of null classes. The Boolean class algebra no longer applies to classes in general, but is reproduced rather within each type. The same is true of the calculus of relations. Even arithmetic, when introduced by definitions on the basis of logic, proves to be subject to the same reduplication. Thus the numbers cease to be unique; a new 0 appears for each type, likewise a new 1, and so on, just as in the case of V and Λ. Not only are all these cleavages and reduplications intuitively repugnant, but they call continually for more or less elaborate technical maneuvers by way of restoring severed connections.

To this objection a variety of replies may be made. One who welcomes the Simple Theory of Types as a true account of the logical nature of things may regard the various duplications as not at all 'unnatural'. They are simply facts to be faced rather than difficulties to be surmounted. But this level of response would seem not to be very fruitful.

Alternatively, we may well challenge the claim that the duplications pointed out are inconvenient. If we make use of typical ambiguity in our notation, a single development of Boolean class algebra suffices for all types by applying to each of them as appropriate type indices are supplied. And the same can be said for arithmetic, even when introduced by definition on the basis of logic.

There are some cleavages, however, and they are certainly inconvenient. Early in Section 1.1 it was remarked that the class of all subclasses of a given class has a higher cardinal number than that of the class itself. This is no longer literally true in the context of the Simple Theory of Types. If a class α is of type τ, its cardinal number is of type $\tau + 1$. Every subclass of α is of type τ, so the class of all of them is of type $\tau + 1$, and *its* cardinal number is of type $\tau + 2$. But cardinal numbers of different types cannot be equal (identical), nor can one be larger than the other. The cleavage can be partially repaired by changing the general theorem to read that the class of all subclasses of a given class has a higher cardinal number than the class of all unit classes of members of the given class. Here we have the desired comparability. But— especially in the context of the system STT with its exclusively homogeneous relations—we cannot establish that there is the same number of members of a class as unit classes of members of that class, for not only are *these* numbers of different types, but any one-one correlating relation between x and $\{x\}$ must be heterogeneous.

A different and very interesting response to this

objection was given by Carnap (1958, 113), who wrote:

> Can this multiplicity of arithmetics be avoided
> without giving up the distinction of types? . . . One
> possible way of avoiding this multiplicity consists
> in adding *transfinite levels*. Using the transfinite
> ordinal numbers of set theory, we designate the
> lowest level that is higher than all the finite levels
> as level ω, the next beyond that as level $\omega + 1$, etc.
> There is then put forward a rule of formation
> specifying that a predicate of any transfinite level
> can take argument-expressions of any lower level
> whatever. . . . If the signs '0', '1', etc., for cardinal
> numbers are assigned level ω, then . . . ['3(F^m)'
> and '3(G^n)' where m $\neq$ n] . . . turn out to be proper
> sentences of the language (and not merely ambiguous
> abbreviations . . .). . . . In this fashion we arrive
> at *one* arithmetic applicable to . . . classes of any
> finite level.

The ingenious device of utilizing transfinite types
serves not only to eliminate duplications of arithmetic
but also to restore 'severed connections', such as that
between the cardinal number of a class and the (higher)
cardinal number of the class of all its subclasses.

There appear to be other advantages to invoking
transfinite types, but it would take us too far afield
to examine them here (Andrews, 1965, x; see also
p. 141 for references to other writings on transfinite
types).

Objection 2   One of the Kneales' objections to the

Simple Theory of Types is that it '... rules out the possibility of providing for the definition of an infinity of natural numbers in any way like that suggested by Frege' (Kneale and Kneale, 1962, 668). This matter was discussed in Section 2.2 in connection with Peano's Axiom 3, and led to the postulating of the axiom of infinity as P7 of $\mathscr{F}^{\mathrm{TT}}$. The Kneales go on to say (*ibid.*, 669) that:

> There is something profoundly unsatisfactory
> about the axiom of infinity. It cannot be described
> as a truth of logic in any reasonable use of that
> phrase, and so the introduction of it as a primitive
> proposition of arithmetic amounts in effect to
> abandonment of Frege's project of exhibiting
> arithmetic as a development of logic.

So much had been admitted by Whitehead and Russell in (1912, II, 183) *Principia Mathematica*, where they said of the axiom of infinity that: 'It seems plain that there is nothing in logic to necessitate its truth or falsehood, and that it can only be legitimately believed or disbelieved on empirical grounds'. It seems clear that this is a serious objection indeed. If the Simple Theory of Types really entails that arithmetic rests on an empirical premiss, then so much the worse for the Theory of Types. There are, after all, other ways to avoid the paradoxes, and the *a priori* nature of arithmetic is surely more evident than any plausibility that may attach to the Simple Theory of Types.

There are several replies, of varying degrees of persuasiveness, that can be made to this objection.

After discussing the problem, Ramsey (1931, 78f) remarked:

> It would appear then impossible to put forward
> analysis except as a consequence of the Axiom of
> Infinity; nor do I see that this would in general be
> objectionable, because there would be little point
> in proving propositions about infinite series unless
> such things existed. And on the other hand the
> mathematics of a world with a given finite number
> of members is of little theoretical interest, as all its
> problems can be solved by a mechanical
> procedure.

I do not find these considerations reassuring, being inclined to think that there are infinite series quite independent of how many individuals there are. Despite these rather light-hearted remarks of Ramsey's, it still seems objectionable to make the truths of mathematics rest upon an empirical premiss.

A more elaborate response makes reference to several important and useful logical systems which embody the Simple Theory of Types but take as their lowest type the set of all natural numbers (Gödel, 1931, system P; Carnap, 1937, Language I and Language II). They thus seem to evade the need for any explicit axiom of infinity. It would appear, however, that this device does away with the need for the axiom of infinity at the cost of abandoning the logistic program of defining the natural numbers in logical terms and deriving arithmetic truths from the truths of logic. A different appraisal of this device is offered by Fraenkel and Bar-Hillel (1958, 167), who follow Carnap in characterizing such systems as '*coordinate-languages*'. They write:

> In such languages, in contradistinction to the more customary *name-languages*, the objects of the fundamental domain are not designated directly by proper names but indirectly by systematic positional coordinates, *i.e.* by symbols that show the place of the objects in the system and thereby their positions in relation to each other. Instead of saying, then, that entity *a*, *i.e.* the entity whose proper name is '*a*', is blue, as customary in name-languages, one says in a coordinate-language that the entity occupying such and such position is blue.

They go on to say, however, that the infinity of entities of the lowest type is not an empirical question (*ibid.*):

> No longer does the statement of infinity assert the existence of infinitely many different particles or other physical entities but rather the fact that the one-dimensional series of positions has no last member, leaving the answer to the question how many of these positions are occupied by physical entities entirely to extra-logical science.
>
> Those authors who are strongly objected against having existence assumptions in logic, whether of an infinity of 'entities' or even of at least one 'entity', seem to have had name-languages in mind; these objections look rather pointless when directed against coordinate-languages, where these 'entities'

are nothing but positions that might well be empty. It appears that the strengthening of the logistic attitude towards the foundations of mathematics entailed by the shift from name to coordinate-languages has not yet been sufficiently taken into account by most authors in this field.

In the first place the coordinate-languages mentioned do *not* get along without any axiom of infinity. Axiom I.2 of Gödel's system P is Peano's Axiom 3, which we have seen to be equivalent to the axiom of infinity (Gödel, 1931, section 2; van Heijenoort, 1967, 599). Peano's Axiom 3 also occurs as Primitive Sentence [Axiom] PS I 10 of Carnap's Language I, and as Primitive Sentence [Axiom] PS II 13 of Carnap's Language II (Carnap, 1937, 30, 92). All that is really being claimed here is that the axiom of infinity is more plausible when asserted of positions than when asserted of objects.

It seems far from clear to me, however, that the existence of infinitely many *positions* is less an empirical question than the existence of infinitely many *objects* occupying such positions. It must not be thought that this device had not been considered by Russell (1919b, 140). He wrote that:

> We have no reason except prejudice for believing in the infinite extent of space and time, at any rate in the sense in which space and time are physical facts, not mathematical fictions. We naturally regard space and time as continuous, or, at least, as compact; but this again is merely prejudice.

And Russell went on to say (*ibid.*, 141) that:

... we must conclude that nothing can be known
a priori as to whether the number of things in the
world is finite or infinite. The conclusion is,
therefore, to adopt a Leibnizian phraseology, that
some of the possible worlds are finite, some infinite,
and we have no means of knowing to which of
these two kinds our actual world belongs. The axiom
of infinity will be true in some possible worlds and
false in others; whether it is true or false in this
world, we cannot tell.

This doctrine of Russell's was vigorously rejected by
Wittgenstein, who maintained in the *Tractatus* that
there are *the same* objects in every possible world
(Wittgenstein, 1922, 2.022, 2.023). Different possible
worlds are simply different configurations of the very
same objects (*ibid.*, 2.027, 2.0271). Hence the number
of objects is *not* a contingent matter, certainly not
an empirical question.

Wittgenstein distinguished in the *Tractatus* between
saying and showing. Only the contingent or *a posteriori*
can be *said*. No *a priori* truths can be pictured (*ibid.*,
2.225), thought (*ibid.*, 3), or said (*ibid.*, 3.1). Propositions of logic are mere tautologies and therefore say
nothing (*ibid.*, 5.43, 6.1, 6.11), and propositions of
mathematics are likewise pseudo-propositions (*ibid.*,
6.2, 6.21). Truths of logic and mathematics must be
shown rather than *said*.

Part of the difficulty is that *object* is a pseudo-
concept: So one cannot say, for example, 'There
are objects', as one might say, 'There are books'.
And it is just as impossible to say, 'There are 100
objects', or, 'There are $\aleph_0$ objects'.

And it is nonsensical to speak of the total number of objects, (*ibid.*, 4.1272).
Since each different name means a different object (*ibid.*, 3.203, 5.53),

> What the axiom of infinity is intended to say would express itself in language through the existence of infinitely many names with different meanings (*ibid.*, 5.535).

Unfortunately for the possibility of arriving at a decision as to the truth or falsehood (*a priori*, of course) of the axiom of infinity, '. . . we are unable to give the number of names with different meanings . . .' (*ibid.*, 5.55).

But from Wittgenstein's point of view in the *Tractatus*, the axiom of infinity is either a tautology or a contradiction, though we cannot tell which. Ramsey agreed with Wittgenstein on this matter, explicating the position in the following terms (Ramsey, 1931, 60f):

> . . . let us take 'There are at least two individuals' or '$(\exists x, y).\ x \neq y$'. This is the logical sum of the propositions $x \neq y$, which are tautologies if x and y have different values, contradictions if they have the same value. Hence it is the logical sum of a set of tautologies and contradictions; and therefore a tautology if any one of the set is a tautology, but otherwise a contradiction. That is, it is a tautology if x and y can take different values (*i.e.* if there are two individuals), but otherwise a contradiction.
> A little reflection will make it clear that this will

hold not merely of 2, but of any other number,
finite or infinite. That is, 'There are at least *n*
individuals' is always either a tautology or a
contradiction, never a genuine proposition. We
cannot, therefore, say anything about the number
of individuals, since, when we attempt to do so, we
never succeed in constructing a genuine proposition,
but only a formula which is either tautological or
self-contradictory. The number of individuals can,
in Wittgenstein's phrase, only be shown, and it
will be shown by whether the above formulae are
tautological or contradictory.

. . . the Axiom of Infinity . . . , if it is a tautology,
cannot be proved, but must be taken as a primitive
proposition. And this is the course which we must
adopt, unless we prefer the view that all analysis
is self-contradictory and meaningless. We do not
have to assume that any particular set of things,
e.g. atoms, is infinite, but merely that there is some
infinite type which we can take to be the type of
individuals.

Two other replies can be made to the objection that
the Simple Theory of Types requires that we postulate
an axiom of infinity. One of them is simply an *ad
hominen*. *Every* effort to formulate a consistent system
of logic adequate to arithmetic requires an axiom of
infinity. As Fraenkel and Bar-Hillel admit, 'From the
axiomatic viewpoint there is no alternative for securing
infinite sets but *postulating* them. . . .' (Fraenkel and
Bar-Hillel, 1958, 82). The other reply is that if transfinite types are adopted as suggested by Carnap, the

enlarged system will permit the definition of infinitely many natural numbers without the adoption of an explicit axiom of infinity. For every natural number n in the transfinite type ω there is a class of type $k \leqslant n$ which belongs to n, even if the lowest type 0 is completely empty. For in that, the least favorable, case, type 1 will contain the null set Λ^1, type 2 will contain 2 members: Λ^2 and $\{\Lambda^1\}$; type 3 will contain 4 members: Λ^3, $\{\Lambda^2\}$, $\{\{\Lambda^1\}\}$, $\{\Lambda^2, \{\Lambda^1\}\}$; and so on. Of course it may be urged that admitting a transfinite type is already to postulate an axiom of infinity. But if one did not put infinity into the system one way or another, one could scarcely hope to find it there.

Objection 3 A frequently expressed objection to the Simple Theory of Types is that it is itself involved in contradiction. The Theory states that nothing can be said about *all* properties, *all* relations, *all* classes, or *all* functions. But to say this the Theory itself must say something about all properties, relations, classes, functions. As Fitch has written (Fitch, 1952, v; see also Gödel, 1944, 149):

> ... a theory of types, if viewed as applying to all
> classes, cannot itself even be stated without
> violating its own principles. Such a statement
> would be concerned with all classes and so would
> be meaningless according to the principles of such
> a theory of types itself.

In the same vein, the Kneales (1962, 670) wrote about the

> ... fundamental difficulty that it seems impossible

71

to formulate the theory without violating its own provisions because words like 'function', 'entity', and 'type' must always remain free from type restrictions. If, for example, we say that no function may be asserted significantly of all entities without distinction of type, our own statement involves the unlimited generality which it declares to be impossible. And again there must be something wrong with any definition of a type according to which two entities are of the same type if a propositional function which can be affirmed or denied significantly of either can also be affirmed or denied significantly of the other. For when we try to apply such a definition in a particular case, and say, for example, that Plato is of the same type as Socrates but wisdom not of the same type, we find ourselves involved in a contradiction. From our pronouncement it follows that Plato is not of the same type as wisdom, and yet the pronounce-ment itself shows clearly that there is at least one function which can be affirmed truly of Plato and denied truly of wisdom, namely being of the same type as Socrates.

Although as early as 1918 Russell had stated unequivocally that 'the theory of types is really a theory of symbols, not of things' (Russell, 1918–19, reprinted in Russell, 1956, 267), he wrote in his 'Reply to Criticisms' in 1944 as follows:

Mr. Black argues that the theory of types, if true, cannot be stated without contradiction. This is a point which formerly troubled me a good deal;

the very word 'type' sinned against the letter of the
theory. But the trouble can be avoided by rewording.
Words, in themselves, are all of the same type; they
are classes of similar series of shapes or noises.
They acquire their type-status through the syntactical
rules to which they are subject. . . . Difference of
type means difference of syntactical functions. Two
words of different types can occur in inverted
commas in such a way that either can replace the
other, but cannot replace each other when the
inverted commas are absent (Russell, 1944, 692).

But one cannot characterize a language by giving an
account, however detailed, of its syntax alone. A
language has a semantical dimension at least as
important as its syntactical one. And when the meaning
relations involved in its semantical rules are formulated,
it will be found that what is said formally about the
linguistic structure must be stated materially about
the interpretation. If the language is one that syn-
tactically embodies the Simple Theory of Types, then
its semantical rules must presuppose or state explicitly
corresponding type distinctions among elements or
aspects of the model in terms of which the language
is interpreted.

The point can be put another way. Suppose the
language in question is governed by a syntactical
rule that prevents admission of a formula like '$x^m \, \epsilon \, y^n$'
except where $m+1 = n$. Then the classes α and β of
any model which can constitute an interpretation of
the language must be subject to exactly analogous
restrictions. Otherwise there will be facts involving
classes α and β of the model that the language in

question will not be adequate to formulate. This phase of the objection has been put very clearly by Fitch (1952, 225):

> One way of attempting to meet the objection . . . is to assert that a formulation of a theory of types is simply the formulation of certain more or less arbitrary or conventional stipulations about the permitted ways of combining symbols. This answer seems to be all right so long as one is restricting oneself to the realm of uninterpreted symbols, but as soon as one enters the realm of semantical concepts it becomes necessary to apply distinctions of 'type' to *meanings* of symbols as well as to symbols themselves . . .

In short, the objection that the Simple Theory of Types cannot be stated without violating its own provisions, is not really answered by the claim that the theory pertains only to symbols, not to things. For when a language embodying a type theory is interpreted, types must be imposed on those things in terms of which the language is being interpreted.

There is another kind of response to the objection that seems to be more satisfactory. In the *Tractatus* Wittgenstein introduces the notion of '. . . a sign-language that excludes . . . [such errors, by being] . . . governed by *logical* grammar—by logical syntax' (Wittgenstein, 1922, 3.325). So far Wittgenstein is not very different from Russell. But Wittgenstein goes on to say that 'The rules of logical syntax must go without saying . . .' (*ibid.*, 3.334). What Wittgenstein *might* have had in mind here, with respect to the Simple Theory of Types, could be something like the following.

In such a logical language the vocabulary might consist of one-inch lengths of metal pipe, of k inch outside diameter ($k = 1, 2, 3, \ldots$), threaded on both their inside and outside surfaces to screw into each other, together with one-inch lengths of metal rod of half-an-inch diameter, threaded to screw into the one-inch outside diameter pipe sections. The translation of the formula '$x \in y$' from STT into this rod and pipe language (RPL) would consist of the result of screwing the rod or pipe section that translates 'x' into the pipe section that translates 'y'. We would need no rule to prevent such formulas as '$x \in x$' or any formula representing an $\in$-cycle from being translated into RPL, because the notation itself prevents their formulation in RPL. The semantics of RPL would consist of correlating its rods with individuals, its sections of one-inch diameter pipe with classes of individuals, and its sections of $k+1$ inch diameter pipe with classes of entities represented by sections of k inch diameter pipe. The language RPL would thus *embody* the Simple Theory of Types so literally as to obviate any need to *state* the theory. This fanciful system RPL is not proposed for actual use as a language, of course. It is intended only to illustrate the way in which a logical doctrine can be realized by a language without having to be stated explicitly. And this, I believe, is at the heart of Wittgenstein's response to the objection that the statement of the Simple Theory of Types must violate its own provisions. We need not state these provisions at all: it suffices to build them into the very structure of the language.

75

Chapter 3
THE RAMIFIED THEORY OF TYPES

The Ramified Theory of Logical Types was first published by Russell in 1908, and was restated without significant modification by Whitehead and Russell in 1910. It was originally called by Russell simply 'The Theory of Types' (1908), and expounded by Whitehead and Russell in Chapter II of the 'Introduction to the First Edition' of *Principia Mathematica* as 'The Theory of Logical Types' (1910). It did not become known as the 'Ramified' or 'Branched' theory until after the Simple Theory of Types had been abstracted from it and developed independently.

The Ramified Theory of Types was proposed as a method of resolving (or avoiding) all of the paradoxes (both logical and semantical). It was also claimed that the theory has 'a certain consonance with common sense which makes it inherently credible' (Russell, 1908, 222; Russell, 1956, 59; Whitehead and Russell, 1910, 37). As initially formulated, however, the Ramified Theory of Types proved to be so restrictive as to prevent the derivation of a great deal of classical mathematics. To ease this excessive restrictiveness Russell added what he called the axiom of reducibility (see Section 3.5 below). But this new axiom was never generally accepted. Today the Ramified Theory of Types with the axiom of reducibility seems to have fallen into complete disfavor. Without the axiom of reducibility, various versions of the Ramified Theory of Types have recently been revived by mathematicians and logicians who adopt a constructivist approach to the development of mathematics. The method generally favored today, for avoiding the semantical paradoxes is the 'levels of language' doctrine (see Section 3.8 below), which is very much like the Ramified Theory of Types, but without any negative implications for the development of mathematics.

3.1 The Vicious Circle Principle

Jules Richard presented his own resolution for the paradox that bears his name (see Section 1.2). The sequence of words that appears to provide a finite definition of the 'diagonal' number N which differs in its nth decimal place from the nth number in the class E of all finitely definable real numbers can define N '. . . only if the set E is totally defined, and this is not done except by infinitely many words' (Richard, 1905). Poincaré applauded Richard's solution and declared that it 'extends, *mutatis mutandis*, to the other like paradoxes' (Poincaré, 1906, 305; 1913, 478). His formulation of Richard's explanation is that:

> E is the aggregate of *all* the numbers definable by a finite number of words, *without introducing the*

77

notion of the aggregate E itself. Else the definition
of *E* would contain a vicious circle; we must not
define *E* by the aggregate *E* itself (Poincaré, 1906,
307; 1913, 480).

Russell had characterized as 'predicative' those norms
or membership conditions which define classes, and
wrote: 'Norms . . . which do not define classes I
propose to call *non-predicative . . .*' (Russell, 1906b,
34). Poincaré amalgamated these two notions, writing:

> Thus *the definitions which should be regarded as
> not predicative are those which contain a vicious
> circle* (Poincaré, 1906, 307; 1913, 481).

In *Principia Mathematica*, which contains his most
complete exposition of the Ramified Theory of Types,
Russell wrote that *all* of the paradoxes (both logical
and semantical, since they were not distinguished until
later), 'result from a certain kind of vicious circle',
and referred to the passage from Poincaré quoted
above. According to Russell, 'The vicious circles in
question arise from supposing that a collection of
objects may contain members which can only be
defined by means of the collection as a whole' (Whitehead and Russell, 1910, 37). Russell explained (*ibid.*,
37) that:

> . . . given any set of objects such that, if we suppose
> the set to have a total, it will contain members
> which presuppose this total, then such a set cannot
> have a total. By saying that a set has no total, we
> mean, primarily, that no significant statement can
> be made about all its members.

Russell offered two additional and more explicit formulations of what he called the 'vicious circle principle' (*ibid.*):

> 'Whatever involves *all* of a collection must not be one of the collection'; or, conversely: 'If, provided a certain collection had a total, it would have members only definable in terms of that total, then the said collection has no total'.

We thus have three formulations of Russell's vicious circle principle, in terms of 'presupposing', 'involving' and 'definable only in terms of'. Or rather, as Gödel has pointed out, 'we have really three different principles', of which only the third version, formulated in terms of 'definability', rules out impredicative or non-predicative definitions (Gödel, 1944, 135). We shall discuss the vicious circle principle further, in Section 3.7, when we consider criticisms of the Ramified Theory of Types.

3.2 The Hierarchy of Propositions

The notion of a *proposition* is not altogether clear in *Principia Mathematica*. The authors of that work had evidently not decided whether a proposition is a sentence (in which the words 'all' or 'some' could be present) (Whitehead and Russell, 1910, 50) or something *expressed* by either a sentence (*ibid.*, 38) or a phrase (*ibid.*, 44). The matter is further complicated by the declaration that 'propositions are incomplete symbols' (*ibid.*). In any event, whichever (or whatever) they are, propositions are said to constitute an 'illegitimate totality', that is, 'a set having no total' (*ibid.*, 37). If there *were* a totality of propositions it would have to contain such members as the proposition that 'all propositions are either true or false'. But such a proposition can be legitimate only if '... "all propositions" referred to some already definite collection, which it cannot do if new propositions are created by statements about "all propositions" ' (*ibid.*). Confronted with such a situation as this, '... it is necessary to break up our set into smaller sets, each of which is capable of a total. This is what the theory of types aims at effecting' (*ibid.*).

We therefore dissolve the illegitimate totality of 'all propositions' into smaller sets, each of which has a total. These are arranged in a hierarchy. The base of the hierarchy consists of all propositions which are not themselves *about* propositions. These are called *first order propositions*. Propositions which are *about* first order propositions but not about any other propositions are *second order propositions*. These are the second tier in the hierarchy. In general, propositions which are *about* *n*th order propositions but not *about* any propositions of order greater than *n* are propositions of order $n+1$.

One proposition is said to be *about* another proposition just in case the sentence or formula expressing the first one contains a bound variable within whose range the second proposition lies. Here we are committed to quantification over propositional variables. But we permit propositional variables to range over *limited* collections of propositions only.

The authors of *Principia Mathematica* go on to

assert that '... the words "true" and "false" have many different meanings, according to the kind of proposition to which they are applied' ... (*ibid.*, 42). To make this explicit we should need to introduce propositional symbols

$$p^m, q^m, r^m, p_1^m, q_1^m, r_1^m, p_2^m, q_2^m, \ldots$$

with $m = 1, 2, 3, \ldots$ Propositional symbols with the same superscript would express propositions of the same order. In presenting the semantics of the system, in place of the two truth values t and f we might well make use of an infinite list of truth values, two truth values t_m and f_m for each order m ($m = 1, 2, 3, \ldots$) (compare Church, 1956, fn. 577).

The hierarchy of propositions permits a satisfactory resolution of all versions of the paradox of the liar. Every version of the liar paradox presents us with a sentence S which predicates falsehood of either *the* proposition or *all* propositions satisfying a certain condition, which the proposition expressed by S alone appears to satisfy. But to refer to the proposition or all propositions satisfying a specified condition, the sentence S must contain a bound propositional variable which ranges over propositions of lower order than the order of the proposition expressed by S itself. Hence no proposition can predicate falsehood of itself and the contradiction vanishes (Whitehead and Russell, 1910, 62; see also Russell, 1918a, Ch. xxxix, 'The Hierarchy of Jokes', reprinted here as Appendix).

Nor is much use made of the hierarchy of propositions. As the authors of *Principia Mathematica* say, it '... is never required in practice, and is only relevant for the solution of paradoxes . . .' (Whitehead and Russell, 1910, 55).

3.3 Simple Type Theory as Part of Ramified Type Theory

The hierarchy of propositions is quite clearly entailed by the vicious circle principle, and does furnish a resolution of the various versions of the liar paradox. But it has no bearing at all on the logical paradoxes. Nor is it of any utility in resolving the other semantical paradoxes, such as those of König, Dixon, Berry, Richard or Grelling. To resolve all these other paradoxes a further hierarchy is required, that of propositional functions.

The Ramified Theory of Types partitions propositional functions in a quite complicated way to take care of the remaining paradoxes. The hierarchy of functions is much more complicated than the hierarchy of propositions. One dimension of this ramified hierarchy of functions divides propositional functions into functions of individuals (functions of type 1), functions of functions of individuals (functions of type 2), and so on. When functions of more than one argument are considered, this one dimension of the hierarchy becomes quite complicated itself. A rough version of the logic embodied in $\mathscr{F}^{\mathrm{TT}}$ is one part of *Principia Mathematica*'s Ramified Theory of Types. One dimension of the Ramified Theory is the Simple Theory of Types, which suffices to avoid the logical paradoxes as explained in Chapter 2.

The other dimension of the Ramified Theory of Types cuts right across the Simple Type Theory. For each type, the functions of that type are divided further into infinitely many *orders*. This will be explained in the following section, where we will see that this dimension of the hierarchy of functions adequately resolves the remaining semantical paradoxes.

As Ramsey observed, the Ramified 'Theory of Types . . . consists really of two distinct parts directed respectively against the two groups of contradictions'. And Ramsey went on to say: 'These two parts were unified by being both deduced in a rather sloppy way from the "vicious circle principle" ' (Ramsey, 1926; 1931, 24, 76). We shall not attempt to reproduce here or to analyse Whitehead and Russell's putative deduction of the Simple Type Theory hierarchy of functions from the vicious circle principle. The Kneales have observed that 'Russell's argument from his vicious-circle principle does nothing to prove that an attribute must always be of the *next* higher type to the entities of which it can be asserted or denied significantly; but this is what he assumes in the development of his theory . . .' (Kneale and Kneale, 1962, 658). Gödel has expressed himself in much stronger terms, writing that: '. . . the simple theory of types . . . in *Principia* is combined with the theory of orders (giving as a result the "ramified hierarchy") but is entirely independent of it and has nothing to do with the vicious circle principle' (Gödel, 1944, 134–5, see also 133, 147)[1].

---

[1] For another account of the connection between the vicious circle principle and the simple type dimension of the ramified hierarchy, see Quine, 1963, Ch. xi, xii.

In any event, regardless of its connection or lack of connection with the vicious circle principle, the Simple Theory of Types is a part of the Ramified Theory of Types in *Principia Mathematica*. And in virtue of containing it as a part, the Ramified Theory of Types manages to avoid all of the logical paradoxes.

3.4 Hierarchies of Orders

After having sketched the hierarchy of types of functions according to the different types of arguments they may take, Whitehead and Russell (1910, 48) state:

> But the hierarchy which has to be constructed is not so simple as might at first appear. The functions which can take *a* as argument form an illegitimate totality, and themselves require division into a hierarchy of functions.

We shall simplify our account of this ramification or branching of each type into orders by confining our attention to propositional functions of one argument. Instead of the enormously complicated panoply of functions whose symbols have all of the type indices used in constructing the system $\mathscr{F}^{\mathrm{TT}}$, let us consider only functions of one argument. These will be represented by predicate symbols with type indices 1, 2, 3, ... The following array of symbols presents a rough 'picture' of the predicates required in this simplified Simple Theory of Types:

$$\begin{matrix} \cdot & & \cdot & & \cdot & & \cdot \\ \cdot & & \cdot & & \cdot & & \cdot \\ \cdot & & \cdot & & \cdot & & \cdot \end{matrix}$$

type 3: F^3, G^3, H^3, ...
type 2: F^2, G^2, H^2, ...
type 1: F^1, G^1, H^1, ...
type 0: a, b, c, ...; x, y, z, ...

Here only a function of type 1 can be significantly predicated of an individual, and only a function of type $n+1$ can be significantly predicated of a function of type n.

Now the Ramified Theory of Types divides each type above the zero level into a further hierarchy. This division of functions of the same type into different *orders* is required by the vicious circle principle. Where G^n is a variable of type n, the formulas '$(F^{n+1})F^{n+1}(G^n)$' and '$(\exists F^{n+1})F^{n+1}(G^n)$' both express functions of type $n+1$. But these expressions contain the bound variable 'F^{n+1}' which ranges over the totality of all functions of type $n+1$. They are definable only in terms of the totality of functions of type $n+1$. So if the collection of functions of type $n+1$ had a total, it would contain members only definable in terms of that total. Hence the collection has no total, and according to the vicious circle principle no significant statement can be made about all functions of any given type.

We therefore dissolve the illegitimate totality of 'all functions of type n' into smaller sets, each of which is capable of a total. These smaller sets of functions of type n are arranged in a hierarchy. The

85

base of the hierarchy consists of all propositional functions which are definable without any reference to any totality of functions of type n. These are called *first order* propositional functions of type n, and we can represent them by

$$^1F^n, \; ^1G^n, \; ^1H^n, \; \ldots \; ^1$$

Next, functions which are definable by reference to the totality of first order propositional functions, or whose expressions contain bound variables ranging over first order propositional functions, are called *second order* propositional functions of type n, and are represented by

$$^2F^n, \; ^2G^n, \; ^2H^n, \; \ldots$$

In general, functions definable by reference to the totality of kth order functions but no totality of functions of order greater than k are of order $k+1$.

Some examples might help to make this hierarchy of orders clear. $^1F^1(x)$ and $(y)[^1F^1(y) \rightarrow {}^1G^1(x)]$ are both first order functions of the argument x. $(^1F^1)[^1G^2(^1F^1) \rightarrow {}^1F^1(x)]$ and $(\exists {}^1F^1)(y)[^1F^1(y) \vee {}^1F^1(x)]$ are both second order functions of x. Since x

---

[1] Some passages of *Principia Mathematica* suggest that the lowest order of those functions which take arguments of type n must be $n+1$. This suggestion seems designed to foster the idea that there is a closer connection between types and orders than really obtains. The relevant nomenclature has not been set forth precisely, and is not consistently followed either in *Principia* or in subsequent writers on type theory. In *Principia* the terms 'type' and 'order' often appear to be used interchangeably. Subsequent development of first order, second order, and higher order functional or predicate calculi have served to confound confusion. Compare Church, 1956, fn. 578.

is of type 0, all four functions are of type 1. The two second order functions could be expressed by the symbols '$^2H_1^1$' and '$^2H_2^1$'.

The Ramified Theory of Types for functions of a single argument can be described or 'pictured' by means of the following array of predicate symbols required in its full development:

	Order 1	Order 2	Order 3	...
	.	.	.	.
	.	.	.	.
	.	.	.	.
	.	.	.	.

type 3: $^1F^3, ^1G^3, ^1H^3,...$; $^2F^3, ^2G^3, ^2H^3,...$; $^3F^3, ^3G^3, ^3H^3,...$; ...
type 2: $^1F^2, ^1G^2, ^1H^2,...$; $^2F^2, ^2G^2, ^2H^2,...$; $^3F^2, ^3G^2, ^3H^2,...$; ...
type 1: $^1F^1, ^1G^1, ^1H^1,...$; $^2F^1, ^2G^1, ^2H^1,...$; $^3F^1, ^3G^1, ^3H^1,...$; ...

Let us now examine the way in which the Hierarchy of Orders of the Ramified Theory of Types prevents the semantical paradoxes. The König, Dixon, Berry and Richard paradoxes all involve numbers (of various kinds) and specifically semantical notions such as 'finite definability', 'specifiability using no more than n symbols' and 'nameability in fewer than k syllables'. It will be convenient to focus our discussion on the Berry paradox, which involves the last notion mentioned (with k set equal to nineteen).

The word 'nameable', according to Whitehead and Russell, 'refers to the totality of names, and yet is allowed to occur in what professes to be one among names' (*ibid.*, 63). So by the vicious circle principle there can be no totality of names, and names must be divided according to their order. For names of objects of a given type, say i, the hierarchy of orders

87

of functions of type $i+1$ operates to divide the names into a corresponding hierarchy of names of different orders. Elementary names, that is, logically proper names not involving any descriptions, do not enter into this hierarchy. First order names of objects of type i are such as involve a description by means of a first order function of type $i+1$, e.g. 'the object (of type i) satisfying the first order function $^1F^{i+1}$'. Second order names of objects of type i are such as involve a description by means of a second order function of type $i+1$, e.g. 'the object satisfying the second order function $^2F^{i+1}$'. Any such name, containing an expression for a second order function, must involve, presuppose or be definable only in terms of the totality of first order functions; and some of them will involve reference to the totality of first order names. And the hierarchy continues, with names of every order within each type. The word 'nameable' is typically ambiguous with respect to order. To resolve the ambiguity we must specify 'nameable by a name of order n'. And any name containing the phrase 'nameable by a name of order n' will be a name of order higher than n. For a suitable choice of k (e.g. 28) we can prove that: the least integer not nameable by a name of order n in fewer than k syllables *is* nameable in fewer than k syllables—but nameable by a name of order $n+1$, not a name of order n. This harmless truism is all that remains of the Berry paradox in the context of the Ramified Theory of Types. The other paradoxes of this kind are similarly resolved by hierarchies of *definitions of order n* and of *specifications of order n*.

The Ramified Theory of Types

It will be instructive to examine a somewhat more formal derivation of the Grelling paradox, patterned after Ramsey's version of it (Ramsey, 1926, 358, 369–72; Ramsey, 1931, 27, 42). We use 'Des' to designate the name relation, and symbolize 's designates F' by 'Des(s,F)'. We assume also the standard convention governing quotation marks, according to which 'Des$('F',F)$' is always true. We begin with the definition:

D. Het(s) for $(\exists F)\{$Des$(s,F) \cdot (G)[$Des$(s,G) \leftrightarrow (G = F)] \cdot \sim F(s)\}$

Now assuming that Het('Het') we derive

(1) $(\exists F)\{$Des$('$Het$',F) \cdot (G)[$Des$('$Het$',G) \leftrightarrow (G = F)] \cdot \sim F('Het')\}$
(2) Des$('$Het$',F) \cdot (G)[$Des$('$Het$',G) \leftrightarrow (G = F)] \cdot \sim F('Het')$
(3) $(G)[$Des$('$Het$',G) \leftrightarrow (G = F)]$
(4) Des$('$Het$',$Het$) \leftrightarrow ($Het$ = F)$
(5) Des$('$Het$',$Het$)$
(6) Het $= F$
(7) $\sim F('$Het$')$
(8) $\sim$Het$('$Het$')$

whence Het('Het') $\rightarrow \sim$ Het('Het').
Next, assuming $\sim$Het('Het') we derive

(1) $\sim(\exists F)\{$Des$('$Het$',F) \cdot (G)[$Des$('$Het$',G) \leftrightarrow (G = F)] \cdot \sim F('Het')\}$
(2) $(F)\sim\{$Des$('$Het$',F) \cdot (G)[$Des$('$Het$',G) \leftrightarrow (G = F)] \cdot \sim F('Het')\}$
(3) $\sim\{$Des$('$Het$',$Het$) \cdot (G)[$Des$('$Het$',G) \leftrightarrow (G = Het)] \cdot \sim$Het$('Het')\}$

89

(4) Des('Het',Het) $\rightarrow$ $\sim\{(G)[\text{Des('Het'},G) \leftrightarrow (G = \text{Het})]\cdot \sim\text{Het('Het')}$

(5) Des('Het',Het)

(6) $\sim\{(G)[\text{Des('Het'},G) \leftrightarrow (G = \text{Het})]\cdot \sim\text{Het('Het')}\}$

(7) $(G)[\text{Des('Het'},G) \leftrightarrow (G = \text{Het})] \rightarrow \text{Het('Het')}$

(8) $(G)[\text{Des('Het'},G) \leftrightarrow (G = \text{Het})]$ (assuming 'Het' univocal)

(9) Het('Het')

whence $\sim\text{Het('Het')} \rightarrow \text{Het('Het')}$, and we have the contradiction $\text{Het('Het')} \leftrightarrow \sim\text{Het('Het')}$.

To embed the Ramified Theory of Types' Hierarchy or Orders in the Simple Theory of Types axiomatized as $\mathscr{F}^{\text{TT}}$ in Section 2.2 we must replace the predicate symbols of $\mathscr{F}^{\text{TT}}$ by predicate symbols having left-hand superscripts indicating the order of the function expressed in addition to the right-hand superscripts indicating the type of the function expressed. We must also impose a further restriction or condition on P5 of $\mathscr{F}$, which was previously stated as: P5 $(F)A \rightarrow \dot{S}_F^G[A]$ provided that no free occurrence of G in A lies within the scope of a quantifier containing F. (The notation '$\dot{S}_F^G[A]$' denotes the result of replacing every free occurrence of F in A by G.) The further restriction on P5 required for the Ramified Theory of Types is: 'and provided that the bound predicate variables in G are all of order lower than the order of F, and the predicate constants and free predicate variables in G are of order no higher than the order of F' (compare Church, 1956, 352).

Now we can indicate exactly how the Ramified Theory of Types avoids the Grelling paradox. In the first part of the derivation, the move from (3) to (4) proceeds via P5 and *Modus Ponens*, with the predicate constant 'Het' replacing the predicate variable 'G' in the matrix of (3). But 'Het' is of higher order than 'G' because a bound 'G' occurs in the definition of 'Het'. The additional restriction on P5 imposed in the Ramified Theory of Types prevents this inference by forbidding the replacement of a predicate variable (in this case 'G') by a predicate constant (in this case 'Het') of higher order. And in the second part of the derivation, the move from (2) to (3) also proceeds via P5 and *Modus Ponens*, with the predicate constant 'Het' replacing the predicate variable 'F' in the matrix of (2). Again, 'Het' is of higher order than 'F' because a bound 'F' occurs in the definition of 'Het', and the same additional restriction on P5 prevents the inference. We shall revert to the Grelling paradox again in Section 3.8 in discussing an alternative resolution of the semantic paradoxes.

It must be noted that the Ramified Theory of Types is strongly nonextensional, because functions of different orders must be distinguished even if they happen to be extensionally equivalent. Finally it should be remarked that the Ramified Theory not only avoids the known logical and semantic paradoxes, but is demonstrably consistent. Proofs of its consistency can be found in Fitch (1938), Lorenzen (1951) and Schütte (1952).

3.5 The Axiom of Reducibility

One serious difficulty with the Ramified Theory of

Types is that on its basis 'only a fraction of classical mathematics can be reconstructed' (Fraenkel and Bar-Hillel, 1958, 152). One of the most obvious victims of the Hierarchy of Orders is the theorem of the Least Upper Bound, which asserts that for any bounded collection of real numbers there is a real number that is the Least Upper Bound (LUB) of the collection, that is, a real number that is not less than any in the collection, and such that any other real number not less than any in the collection is greater than it. Mathematicians generally operate with one or another variant of Dedekind's definition of a real number as the class of all ratios or rational numbers less than all rationals that satisfy a specified condition, e.g. the real number $\sqrt{2}$ is the class of all rational numbers less than all rational numbers whose squares are greater than 2. In a Ramified Type Theory the corresponding real number is defined to be the function of rationals satisfied by all and only those rationals less than all rationals whose squares exceed 2. Now given any collection of real numbers G^i that satisfy some condition F^{i+1} and which are bounded, that is, all less than some specified real number G_B^i, it is easy to establish that the indicated real numbers have an LUB. The standard procedure is to define their LUB as the set of all rationals H^{i-1} that belong to any real number G^i satisfying the condition F^{i+1}. The LUB is the function G_{LUB}^i satisfied by all rationals H^{i-1} that are less than all rationals H^{i-1} not belonging to any of the real numbers G^i satisfying F^{i+1}. In symbols, we have the definition

The Ramified Theory of Types

D[LUB] $G^i_{\text{LUB}}(H^{i-1})$ for $(H_1^{i-1})\{(G^i)[F^{i+1}(G^i) \to \sim G^i(H_1^{i-1})] \to (H^{i-1} < H_1^{i-1})\}$

But here the LUB G^i_{LUB} must be of order higher than the order of the real numbers whose LUB it is, because in its definition the bound variable 'G^i' occurs, ranging over all the real numbers satisfying the condition F^{i+1}. So the LUB of a collection of real numbers is of a higher order and cannot serve the mathematical purposes which have made the LUB theorem so central in analysis.

Other ways in which the Ramified Theory of Types amputates major parts of mathematics will be more briefly indicated. It is obvious that the principle of mathematical induction

$$(F)\{\{F(0)\cdot(n)\{N(n) \to [F(n) \to F(n+1)]\}\} \to (n)[N(n) \to F(n)]\}$$

cannot be stated in its full generality for *every* property or function F of natural numbers, but only for all first order properties or all second order properties or etc. (see Russell, 1908, Pt. V; Russell, 1956, 80f). Not only is the ordinary arithmetic of natural numbers diminished by the Ramified Theory of Types, but transfinite arithmetic is also seriously affected. In the general proof of Cantor's fundamental theorem that a class is always smaller than the class of all of its subclasses, the subclass left out of any one-one correlation of members with subclasses is specified impredicatively. In terms of the Ramified Theory, we consider the collection of objects x satisfying a given function M, and consider the various distinct functions

93

F satisfied only by objects x that satisfy M. In considering any one-one correlation of objects in M with such functions, we follow Cantor in specifying a function that is left out of the correlation by defining

D. $W(x)$ for $M(x) \cdot (F)\{(y)[F(y) \to M(y)] \to$
$[\text{Corr}_{1-1}(x, F) \to \sim F(x)]\}$

But in the context of the Hierarchy of Orders the proof does not establish that one of the given F's has been left out of the one-one correlation. In the definition of the function W a bound predicate 'F' occurs, so W is of order higher than the order of the given F's. No matter what order j of functions F we consider, all that Cantor's proof establishes is that given any one-one correlation of members x with functions F of order j, there is a function of higher order $j+1$ which is not included in the correlation. But for this we scarcely need an argument.

Another objection to the Ramified Theory of Types is that it prevents our defining identity of objects a^i and b^i of type i by the formula $(F^{i+1})[F^{i+1}(a^i) \leftrightarrow F^{i+1}(b^i)]$. There is no totality of functions of type $i+1$ over which the variable 'F^{i+1}' can range. There are different orders of functions of each type, and a variable can range over just one order. (Of course, since $(^jF^{i+1})[^jF^{i+1}(a^i) \leftrightarrow {}^jF^{i+1}(x)]$ is a function of x of order $j+1$, to assert that $(^jF^{i+1})[^jF^{i+1}(a^i) \leftrightarrow {}^jF^{i+1}(b^i)]$ is to assert that a^i and b^i share all their properties of every order up to order j.) Two entities a^i and b^i may agree in all their properties of orders 1, 2, 3, $\ldots$, j and still differ with respect to some property of order $j+1$, and therefore not be identical.

94

The Ramified Theory of Types

To ease these excessive restrictions of the Ramified Theory of Types Russell introduced a new and special axiom, the axiom of reducibility. It is really a multiply infinite set of axioms: for each type i ($i = 1, 2, 3, \ldots$) there are axioms of reducibility:

$$(\exists^1 F^i)(G^{i-1})[{}^j F^i(G^{i-1}) \leftrightarrow {}^1 F^i(G^{i-1})]$$
$$(\exists^1 F^i)(G_1^{i-1})(G_2^{i-1})[{}^j F^i(G_1^{i-1}, G_2^{i-1}) \leftrightarrow {}^1 F^i(G_1^{i-1}, G_2^{i-1})]$$
$$(\exists^1 F^i)(G_1^{i-1})(G_2^{i-1})(G_3^{i-1})[{}^j F^i(G_1^{i-1}, G_2^{i-2}, G_3^{i-1}) \leftrightarrow$$
$$ {}^1 F^i(G_1^{i-1}, G_2^{i-1}, G_3^{i-1})]$$

. . . .

where ${}^1 F^i$ is a first order function and ${}^j F^i$ is a formally or extensionally equivalent function of arbitrary order $j > 1$. The axiom of reducibility asserts that for any function of any type, any order, and of any number of arguments, there is a formally equivalent function of the same type and the same number of arguments but of the first order. (First order functions are called 'predicative functions' in *Principia Mathematica*, and are distinguished not by the superscript '1', as here, but by having an exclamation point between the function symbol and its arguments. What appears here as '${}^1 F(x)$' or '${}^1 G(x, y)$' would appear in *Principia* as '$F!x$' or '$G!(x, y)$'.)

Having assumed the axiom of reducibility, we find that the onerous restrictions of the Ramified Theory of Types are greatly eased. It is possible to define identity in terms of first order functions:

$$D[=] \ G^i = H^i \text{ for } ({}^1 F^{i+1})[{}^1 F^{i+1}(G^i) \leftrightarrow {}^1 F^{i+1}(H^i)].$$

For if G^i satisfies a higher order function ${}^j F^{i+1}$, there is a first order function ${}^1 F^{i+1}$ that G^i also satisfies

95

(by the axiom of reducibility), and by the given definition of identity, H^i also satisfies that first order function $^1F^{i+1}$, and by the formal equivalence of $^1F^{i+1}$ and $^jF^{i+1}$, H^i satisfies the latter also. Similarly, it now will suffice to state the principle of mathematical induction in terms of first order properties only, because the axiom of reducibility draws all higher order properties in the wake of the first order ones. The Least Upper Bound theorem is restored, because to the higher order function $^jG^i_{LUB}$ there corresponds the predicative function $^1G^i_{LUB}$ which is a real number like the others. And Cantor's theorem is similarly restored, because to the higher order (subset) function $W(x)$ that is not correlated with any x there is a formally equivalent first order function ^1F_W that is not correlated and must be one of the given F's.

3.6 Criticisms of the Axiom of Reducibility

The question naturally arises: does the axiom of reducibility ease the restrictions of the Ramified Theory of Types sufficiently to reinstate the semantic paradoxes? At one time Chwistek (1922) thought that it did reinstate the Richard paradox. But his argument was defective in that not sufficient heed was paid to the radical nonextensionality of the Ramified Theory of Types, in which distinct functions can be formally equivalent. A higher order function may be 'finitely definable', 'specifiable using no more than n symbols' or 'nameable in fewer than k symbols' and be formally equivalent to a first order function that lacks these semantic characteristics, as pointed out by Ramsey (1926). It is more plausible to try to reinstate the Grelling paradox (Copi, 1950). But for that attempt to succeed the Ramified Theory of Types would have to be expanded to include not only the whole panoply of semantical notions, but also *names* for all relevant predicative functions whose existence is asserted by the axiom of reducibility. It is clearly impossible to name all first order functions corresponding to the real numbers, because of their nondenumerability. So quite impossible general assumptions, or quite unplausible specific assumptions, would have to be made before the reducibility axiom could be claimed to reinstate the Grelling paradox.

But the axiom of reducibility has been subjected to other kinds of criticism. Russell attempted to forestall (or at least anticipate) such criticism by admitting: 'That the axiom of reducibility is self-evident is a proposition which can hardly be maintained' (Whitehead and Russell, 1910, 59). Russell then urged its acceptance on the basis of 'inductive evidence'. But many writers have vigorously criticized and rejected the axiom. Wittgenstein maintained that: 'Propositions like Russell's "axiom of reducibility" are not logical propositions, and this explains our feeling that, even if they were true, their truth could only be the result of a fortunate accident'. He went on to say: 'It is possible to imagine a world in which the axiom of reducibility is not valid. It is clear, however, that logic has nothing to do with the question whether our world really is like that or not' (Wittgenstein, 1922, 6.1232 and 6.1233). Ramsey wrote of it: 'This axiom there is no reason to suppose true; and if it were true, this would be a happy accident and not a logical necessity, for it is not a tautology', and went on to say: 'Such an axiom has no place in mathematics, and anything which cannot be proved without using it cannot be regarded as proved at all' (Ramsey, 1926, 21; 1931, 28). Chwistek followed Poincaré in branding the axiom of reducibility as 'a typical synthetic *a priori* proposition', and wrote: 'If logic were based upon such axioms, it could not be regarded as a science which is independent of metaphysics' (Chwistek, 1948, 157).

In 1925, in the 'Introduction to the Second Edition' of *Principia Mathematica*, Russell discussed the axiom of reducibility again. He admitted that improvement in this area was obviously desirable, for although the axiom has a pragmatic justification, '... clearly it is not the sort of axiom with which we can rest content' (Whitehead and Russell, 1925, p. xiv). He considered as an alternative to it Wittgenstein's suggestion that all functions are extensional, and attempted to make it plausible in Appendix C (*ibid.*, 659–66). In place of the axiom of reducibility he offered the 'fundamental assumption' that '*A function can only occur in a matrix through its values*' (*ibid.*, p. xxix), which is roughly equivalent to saying that functions can occur as arguments only to the truth functional operators '|', '∼', '∨', '·', '⊃', '≡', etc. All formally equivalent, that is, extensionally equivalent, functions *of the same order* are identical. In the context of this assumption he offered a proof of mathematical induction without assuming the axiom of reducibility in Appendix B (*ibid.*, 650–8).[1] But he was unable to find any way to develop either the theory of real numbers (classical analysis) or transfinite arithmetic without the axiom of reducibility. It certainly seems to follow, regardless of Wittgenstein's extensionality suggestion, that if the axiom of reducibility is not accepted, then the Ramified Theory of Types of *Principia Mathematica* cannot be regarded as providing a satisfactory logical basis for mathematics. Ramsey therewith turned his back upon the Ramified Type Theory, writing, 'For as I can neither accept the Axiom of Reducibility nor reject ordinary analysis, I cannot believe in a theory which presents me with no third possibility' (Ramsey, 1926, 22; 1931, 29).

3.7 Criticisms of the Ramified Theory of Types

Even apart from the controversial axiom of reducibility, the Ramified Theory of Types has been subjected to searching criticism.

Fitch has criticized both the Simple and the Ramified Theories of Types. Two of his criticisms seem to apply primarily to the latter, which includes the Hierarchy of Propositions discussed in Section 3.2. One criticism

[1] Much later Gödel pointed out a mistake in the proof of its main lemma, which rendered the proof 'certainly not conclusive' (Gödel, 1944, 145f). Gödel went on to remark that 'the question whether (or to what extent) the theory of integers can be obtained on the basis of the ramified hierarchy must be considered as unsolved at the present time'. But in the 1950s Skolem devised a method of procedure which made him confident that 'a purely logical development of arithmetic similar to that given by Dedekind . . . is possible even in the ramified type theory' (Skolem, 1962, 60).

is that a logic containing a Ramified Theory of Types is 'of little or no use in philosophy'. Fitch maintains that 'philosophy must be free to make completely general statements'. For a philosophical theory to be completely general it must deal with theories, among other things, and must therefore be self-referential in a way that the Ramified Theory prohibits. Another criticism is that type theory rules out as 'meaningless' some philosophically important types of arguments which involve propositions that have the character of referring directly or indirectly to themselves. What Fitch seems to have in mind here is the sort of *ad hominem* argument which purports to find a 'self-referential inconsistency' in the view being argued against. One of Fitch's examples is the solipsist who argues for his view, for a solipsist 'might be expected to hold the view that his solipsism needs no defense against the attack of an opponent, since the solipsist maintains that nobody else, and hence no opponent, exists' (Fitch, 1952, p. v, 217–25).

These criticisms of type theory seem based upon the belief that the theory in question was proposed as a modification of or an improvement upon ordinary language. It must be confessed that some of Russell's formulations invite this interpretation. For example, Russell (Whitehead and Russell, 1910, 38) wrote that:

> ... the imaginary sceptic, who asserts that he knows nothing, and is refuted by being asked if he knows that he knows nothing, has asserted nonsense, and has been fallaciously refuted by an argument that involves a vicious-circle fallacy.

But as was said before, in Section 2.1, the theories of types must not be thought of as either descriptive of or prescriptive for ordinary language. They are offered, and must be regarded as, specifications for artificial languages that will optimally serve specific purposes. These purposes are generally scientific, and more particularly mathematical. These purposes are not sufficiently well served by ordinary language, as is shown by the various jargons and technical notations developed in the advancing sciences. Part of the reason, it may be claimed, why ordinary language is not an altogether satisfactory instrument for developing mathematics is its excessively self-referential capabilities, which permit the derivation of contradictions within it. Of course that capability may contribute to its usefulness for other purposes. But it must not be thought that the Theory of Types eliminates *all* self-reference. The language whose syntax was arithmetized by Gödel to permit a formula to state its own non-provability is a language embodying the Simple Theory of Types (Gödel, 1931). This is only part, but an important part, of Popper's argument against too facile and simplistic a banishment of self-reference from language, either ordinary or artificial (Popper, 1954, 162–9; Popper, 1963, 304–11). In any event, it is clear that the Simple Theory of Types does not eliminate all self-referential capabilities from languages governed by it. Whether it eliminates so much as to prevent the philosophical arguments prized by Fitch is not easily established. The Ramified Theory of Types, without the reducibility axiom, does seem to do so. But the theory must be judged in terms of its purpose: it was never proposed that *Principia Mathematica* should replace ordinary language for all purposes, not even for all philosophical purposes.

Two early papers by Quine deal critically with the Ramified Type Theory, especially in connection with the axiom of reducibility. In 1936 he offered a 'more formal consideration in support of Ramsey's standpoint', which was to accept only 'the system of *P.M.* minus the second part of the theory of types'. Quine argued that if the axiom of reducibility of the first edition *and* the partial extensionality principle of the second edition were *both* assumed, the effect would be to make the system 'indistinguishable from what that of *P.M.* would have been if the distinction of orders had not been invented'. For by the axiom of reducibility, for any function of any order there is a formally equivalent predicative function, and by the partial extensionality principle which identifies formally equivalent functions of the same order, there is only one such predicative function. Now if we construe every expression for a non-predicative function ϕ of whatever order as denoting rather the predicative function which is formally equivalent to ϕ, the result is the system of *P.M.* with Simple Type Theory but without any partitioning of functions into orders (Quine, 1936).

In 1941 Quine referred to this 1936 paper as part of his justification for saying that 'The whole ramification, with the axiom of reducibility, calls simply for amputation'. The other part of Quine's justification for this conclusion is more persuasive, but it is not new. It is simply a reaffirmation of the Peano-Ramsey view (see Section 1.3) that 'the contradictions against which this part of type theory was directed are no business of logic anyway; they can arise only in discourse that goes beyond pure logic and imports semantic terms such as "true" or "designates" ' (Quine, 1941, 150; Quine, 1966a, 25). The reason why I find Quine's 1936 argument unpersuasive is that at no time did the authors of *Principia Mathematica* ever adopt *both* the partial extensionality principle *and* the axiom of reducibility. Had they done so, however, Quine's criticism would have been decisive.

The Ramified Theory of Types has also been criticized on the basis of its connection—or lack of connection—with the vicious circle principle. As the Kneales remark, '... the principle is dubious and difficult to apply' (Kneale, 1962, 666). It has been objected that some of the specifications ruled out as impredicative on the basis of that principle really do not violate it. The implication here is that the Ramified Theory of Types goes beyond the restrictions actually imposed by the vicious circle principle. Thus Ramsey observes that '... we may refer to a man as the tallest in a group, thus identifying him by means of a totality of which he is himself a member without there being any vicious circle' (Ramsey, 1926, 31; 1931, 41). From the other direction, it has been objected that the Ramified Type Theory—at least in *Principia Mathematica*—does not sufficiently accord with that principle. Having distinguished three forms of the vicious circle principle, Gödel identified the first form as stating: 'no totality can contain members definable only in

H

terms of this totality', and went on to say (Gödel, 1944, 135):

> It is the first form which is of particular interest, because only this one makes impredicative definitions impossible and thereby destroys the derivation of mathematics from logic, effected by Dedekind and Frege, and a good deal of modern mathematics itself. It is demonstrable that the formalism of classical mathematics does not satisfy the vicious circle principle in its first form, since the axioms imply the existence of real numbers definable in this formalism only by reference to all real numbers. Since classical mathematics can be built up on the basis of *Principia* (including the axiom of reducibility), it follows that even *Principia* (in the first edition) does not satisfy the vicious circle principle in the first form, if 'definable' means 'definable within the system' and no methods of defining outside the system (or outside other systems of classical mathematics) are known except such as involve still more comprehensive totalities than those occurring in the systems.

> I would consider this rather as a proof that the vicious circle principle is false than that classical mathematics is false, and this is indeed plausible also on its own account. For, first of all one may, on good grounds, deny that reference to a totality necessarily implies reference to all single elements of it ...

Quine has questioned the vicious circle principle

itself, and the proscription of impredicative definitions and specifications that it apparently entails (Quine, 1963, 242):

> And what now of the vicious circle? A circular argument seduces its victim into granting a thesis, unawares, as a premiss to its own demonstration. A circular definition smuggles the definiendum into the definiens, in such wise as to prevent expansion into primitive notation. But impredicative specification of classes is neither of these things. It is hardly a procedure to look askance at, except as one is pressed by the paradoxes to look askance at something or other.

Efforts to defend the vicious circle principle lead in a very interesting direction. Fraenkel and Bar-Hillel consider and criticize four arguments intended to justify it: first, it avoids the semantic paradoxes (*but* there are other ways of doing so); second, it rules out self-reference (*but* self-reference by itself is unobjectionable, as witness the highly useful self-reference in Gödel's arithmetization of syntax); third, it avoids the infinite regression entailed in testing the applicability of impredicative concepts (*but* that is not really entailed, for finite proof procedures often suffice to determine the applicability of impredicative concepts). Only the fourth argument seems plausible: it 'refers to the non-constructive character of impredicatively introduced objects' (Fraenkel and Bar-Hillel, 1958, 176ff).

Here we enter the arena of philosophical interpretation. The Platonist view is that mathematical entities have an independent and timeless existence. The nominalist or conceptualist position is that mathematical entities are human products and exist only after having been 'constructed'. A Platonist can accept impredicative definitions with equanimity; a constructivist must regard them as abhorrent. As Gödel (1944, 136; see also Bernays, 1946) explained:

... the vicious circle principle in its first form applies only if the entities involved are constructed by ourselves. In this case there must clearly exist a definition (namely the description of the construction) which does not refer to a totality to which the object defined belongs, because the construction of a thing can certainly not be based on a totality of things to which the thing to be constructed itself belongs. If, however, it is a question of objects that exist independently of our constructions, there is nothing in the least absurd in the existence of totalities containing members, which can be described (*i.e.*, uniquely characterized) only by reference to this totality.

Some recent efforts to develop mathematics from a constructivist approach lead in the direction of Ramified Type Theories very different from that of *Principia Mathematica*. They operate with orders alone and contain no analogue of the Simple Theory of Types, nor do they seem to require an axiom of reducibility. The motivation for such efforts was most lucidly expounded by Quine in 1953 (Quine, 1953, 102–29). Independent results along this line have been obtained by Hao Wang (1950; 1954) and Paul Lorenzen

(1955). Both are discussed by Fraenkel and Bar-Hillel (1958, 153–60) and Lorenzen by Skolem (1962, 61–4). We can do no better than to conclude this section by quoting Fraenkel and Bar-Hillel's remarks (1958, 160) that:

> The fact that Wang and Lorenzen, starting from quite different backgrounds, the one from a Russell-Zermelo tradition, the other from a constructivist Hilbertism, converge to systems which have so much in common cannot but bring their streamlined version of the ramified type theory back into the race. The old animadversions against this theory do not hold any more.

3.8 An Alternative Resolution of the Semantic Paradoxes

The most widely accepted resolution of the semantic paradoxes today is based upon the distinction between (object) language and metalanguage, generalized to a hierarchy of levels of language: language, meta-language, meta-metalanguage, and so on. Most extensively developed by Tarski (1956, 152–278), it had its historical root in an idea suggested by Russell (1922, 23):

> These difficulties suggest to my mind some such possibility as this: that every language has, as Mr. Wittgenstein says, a structure concerning which, *in the language*, nothing can be said, but that there may be another language dealing with the structure of the first language, and having

itself a new structure, and that to this hierarchy
of languages there may be no limit.

An essential part of what we shall call the 'levels of
language' doctrine is that semantical predicates, such
as 'true', 'false', 'designates', etc., for the terms and
formulas of a given language L can not consistently
be defined or introduced into that language L itself,
but can occur only in the metalanguage for L.

The Kneales have argued that this need to distinguish
among languages of different levels can be derived
from the Simple Theory of Types. They consider the
sentence

'Designates' designates designates,

which attempts to state what 'designates' designates.
Here we have an obvious violation of the Simple
Theory of Types, with a relation purporting to be
one of its own relata (Kneale and Kneale, 1962, 665).
This may well be what Gödel had in mind when he
stated that the Simple Theory of Types avoids the
semantic paradoxes (Gödel, 1944, 134, fn. 17).

It will be useful to indicate briefly how the levels of
language doctrine manages to avoid the semantical
paradoxes, for it will show that the method makes it
very similar to the Ramified Theory of Types[1]. Confining our attention to the Grelling paradox, we note
that it does not arise in an object language (like $\mathscr{F}^{\text{TT}}$,
for example) when we assume that it contains no

---

[1] The remainder of this section is reprinted from 'The
Inconsistency or Redundancy of *Principia Mathematica*',
Philosophy and Phenomenological Research, vol. 11 (1950), by
permission of the University of Buffalo.

symbols which designate symbols. Nor does it arise in the metalanguage of that object language. Since the metalanguage contains synonyms for all symbols of the object language and names for all symbols of the object language, as well as its own variables and the name relation (which we write as 'Des'), the symbol 'Het' can be defined in it. We define:

D. $\text{Het}(s)$ for $(\exists F)\{\text{Des}(s,F) \cdot (G)[\text{Des}(s,G) \leftrightarrow (G = F)] \cdot \sim F(s)\}.$

But the Grelling paradox cannot be derived in the metalanguage, because although it contains a symbol for the function Het it contains no symbol for the name of that function. In other words, in the metalanguage, although we could substitute 'Het' for 'F' we cannot substitute "Het" for 's' because "Het" is not a symbol of the metalanguage.

So far there are no complications. The paradox does not arise in the object language because it contains no names for the symbols in it; and it does not arise in the metalanguage because there is no name for the function symbol 'Het' in that language. The *threat* of the Grelling paradox arises only in the meta-metalanguage. *If* certain safeguards or refinements of the levels of language doctrine are ignored, the paradox seems to be derivable. Ignoring those safeguards, we would have the following definitionally true biconditional in the meta-metalanguage:

$$\text{Het}(s) \leftrightarrow (\exists F)\{\text{Des}(s,F) \cdot (G)[\text{Des}(S,G) \leftrightarrow (G = F)] \cdot \sim F(s)\}.$$

Since the meta-metalanguage *does* contain a name for

the function symbol 'Het', we substitute that name, "Het", for the variable '*s*' and obtain a contradiction just as in the derivation in Section 3.4.

The way in which the safeguards of the levels of language doctrine serve to prevent this contradiction makes it very similar to the Ramified Type Theory's hierarchy of orders. The definition of the function Het in the meta-metalanguage requires the insertion of subscripts to resolve an ambiguity in it. Once the ambiguity is identified and removed, the contradiction vanishes.

In the first place, the meta-metalanguage must contain *two* symbols for name relations, 'Des$_1$' and 'Des$_2$' (as suggested in Ramsey, 1926, 370; 1931, 43). The first is the meta-metalanguage's synonym for the name relation in the metalanguage. The full sentence

$$(1) \qquad \text{Des}_1(s,F)$$

expresses that the function symbol denoted by '*s*' is a symbol of the object language and designates the function *F*. The second, 'Des$_2$', has no synonym in the metalanguage. The full sentence

$$(2) \qquad \text{Des}_2(s,F)$$

expresses that the function symbol denoted by '*s*' is a symbol of the metalanguage and designates the function *F*. These are quite different. If the object language and metalanguage are entirely distinct, the arguments '*s*' in (1) and (2) above have completely different ranges. If the object language is conceived to be nested or embedded in the metalanguage, then the range of '*s*' in (2) is larger than and contains the range of '*s*' in (1).

And in the second place, the meta-metalanguage contains two symbols 'Het$_1$' and 'Het$_2$' whose meanings must be distinguished. The first of these symbols is the meta-metalanguage's synonym for the function symbol 'Het' of the metalanguage. The full sentence

$$\text{Het}_1(s)$$

expresses that the function symbol denoted by '*s*' is a symbol of the object language and has the property of designating in the object language a property which it does not possess. The second of these symbols has no synonym in the metalanguage. The full sentence

$$\text{Het}_2(s)$$

expresses that the function symbol denoted by '*s*' is a symbol of the metalanguage and has the property of designating in the metalanguage a property which it does not possess. Their definitions are different:

D. $\text{Het}_1(s)$ for $(\exists F)\{\text{Des}_1(s,F)\cdot(G)[\text{Des}_1(s,G) \leftrightarrow (G = F)]\cdot {\sim}F(s)\}$

and

D. $\text{Het}_2(s)$ for $(\exists F)\{\text{Des}_2(s,F)\cdot(G)[\text{Des}_2(s,G) \leftrightarrow (G = F)]\cdot {\sim}F(s)\}$

It is clear that we cannot define Het$_1$ in terms of Des$_2$, because the values of the arguments of the two functions are terms of different languages, of the object language for Het$_1$ and of the metalanguage for Des$_2$. The same consideration shows that Het$_2$ cannot be defined in terms of Des$_1$.

No version of the Grelling paradox can be derived from the definition of Het_1, because the only values of its arguments are terms of the object language, and there is no term of the object language analogous to either 'Het_1' or 'Het_2'. The only possibility lies in the direction of deriving a contradiction from the definition of Het_2. And this is thwarted by something remarkably like *Principia Mathematica*'s hierarchy of orders.

In the definition of Het_2 we cannot substitute for 's' the name of the symbol for that function, because although the function symbol 'Het_2' occurs in the meta-language, no *name* of that function symbol does. The best we can do is to substitute the meta-meta-language's name of the function symbol of the metalanguage that is synonymous with 'Het_1', for which we *do* have a name in the meta-metalanguage (call it "Het"). Making the substitution in the definitionally true biconditional, we have

$$Het_2(\text{'Het'}) \leftrightarrow (\exists F)\{Des_2(\text{'Het'}, F) \cdot (G)[Des_2(\text{'Het'}, G) \leftrightarrow (G = F)] \cdot \sim F(\text{'Het'})\}$$

If we try to deduce a contradiction from this biconditional using an argument parallel to earlier versions, we are unable to do so. There is a choice of function symbols to substitute for the bound variable 'G'. Two function symbols in our meta-metalanguage look promising: 'Het_1' and 'Het_2'.

If we substitute 'Het_1' we obtain

$$Het_2(\text{'Het'}) \leftrightarrow \{Des_2(\text{'Het'}, F) \cdot [Des_2(\text{'Het'}, Het_1) \leftrightarrow (Het_1 = F)] \cdot \sim F(\text{'Het'})\}$$

112

"Het" is the meta-metalanguage's name for the function symbol of the metalanguage that is synonymous with 'Het$_1$' so we have

$$\text{Des}_2(\text{'Het'}, \text{Het}_1)[\text{Des}_2(\text{'Het'}, \text{Het}_1) \leftrightarrow (\text{Het}_1 = F)]$$

and consequently

$$\text{Het}_2(\text{'Het'}) \leftrightarrow \sim \text{Het}_1(\text{'Het'}).$$

But this is no part of any contradiction, being antecedently known on independent grounds; for if any term satisfies Het_2 it is in the metalanguage and not in the object language, whereas only terms of the object language satisfy Het_1.

On the other hand, if we substitute 'Het$_2$' we obtain

$$\text{Het}_2(\text{'Het'}) \leftrightarrow \{\text{Des}_2(\text{'Het'}, F) \cdot [\text{Des}_2(\text{'Het'}, \text{Het}_2) \leftrightarrow$$
$$(\text{Het}_2 = F)] \cdot \sim F(\text{'Het'})\}$$

From this, *if* 'Des$_2$('Het', Het$_2$)' were true, we should indeed be able to obtain a contradiction. But 'Des$_2$('Het', Het$_2$)' is *not* true, because the argument "Het" denotes a symbol of the metalanguage whereas the property denoted by the argument 'Het$_2$' is not denoted by any symbol of the metalanguage. In other words, 'Des$_2$('Het', Het$_2$)' is false because 'Het$_2$' is a symbol of the meta-metalanguage which has no synonym in the metalanguage.

This is very much like the Ramified Type Theory's hierarchy of orders, because the contradiction is evaded by arranging that certain symbols of the meta-metalanguage are defined *over certain ranges*. Thus 'Des$_1$' is defined over a narrower range than

113

'Des_2', and 'Het_1' is defined over a narrower range than 'Het_2'; Des_1 and Het_1 being satisfied only by symbols of the object language, Des_2 and Het_2 being satisfied only by symbols of the metalanguage, which is a wider and more inclusive language. Not only is the levels of language doctrine remarkably analogous to the hierarchy of orders, but where each metalanguage is conceived as actually containing the object language with which it deals (Tarski, 1944, 350; 1949, 60–1), it can be identified with Russell's hierarchy of orders *as applied to symbols* rather than to the functions denoted by them.

In spite of the indicated similarity, there are fundamental differences between the two theories under comparison. Most significant is that, unlike *Principia Mathematica*'s Ramified Type Theory, the levels of language doctrine does not jeopardize the derivation of any parts of classical mathematics. So no need arises for any analogue to the axiom of reducibility.

Incidentally, what the Kneales' improper sentence

'Designates' designates designates

was intended to express can be expressed unobjectionably as

$$Des_2('Des', Des_1).$$

Appendix
THE HIERARCHY OF JOKES[1]

Jokes may be divided into various types. Thus a joke
or class of jokes can only be the subject of a joke of
higher order. Otherwise we would get the same
vicious-circle fallacy which gives rise to so many
paradoxes in logic and mathematics. A certain Oxford
scholar succeeded, to his own satisfaction, in reducing
all jokes to primitive types, consisting of thirty-seven
proto-Aryan jokes. When any proposition was pro-
pounded to him, he would reflect and afterwards
pronounce on the question as to whether the proposition was a joke or not. If he decided, by his theory,
that it was a joke, he would solemnly say: 'There *is*
that joke'. If this narration is accepted as a joke,
since it cannot be reduced to one of the proto-Aryan
jokes under pain of leading us to commit a vicious-
circle fallacy, we must conclude that there is at least
one joke which is not proto-Aryan; and, in fact, is
of a higher type. There is no great difficulty in forming
a hierarchy of jokes of various types. Thus a joke of
the fourth type (or order) is as follows: A joke of the

[1] Chapter XXXIX of *The Philosophy of Mr. B*rtr*nd
R*ss*ll*, edited by P. E. B. Jourdain (London and Chicago,
1918a). Reprinted by kind permission of George Allen &
Unwin Ltd, London, and The Open Court Publishing
Company, La Salle, Illinois.

first order was told to a Scotsman, who, as we would expect, was unable to see it.[1]

The person (*A*) who told this joke told the story of how the joke was received to another Scotsman thereby making a joke about a joke of the first order, and thus making a joke of the second order. *A* remarked on this joke that no joke could penetrate the head of the Scotsman to whom the joke of the first order was told, even if it were fired into his head with a gun. The Scotsman, after severe thought, replied: 'But ye couldn't do that, ye know!' *A* repeated the whole story, which constituted a joke of the third order, to a third Scotsman. This last Scotsman again, after prolonged thought, replied: 'He had ye there!' This whole story is a joke of the fourth order.

Most known jokes are of the first order, for the simple reason that the majority of people find that the slightest mental effort effectually destroys any perception of humour. It seems to me that a joke becomes more pleasurable in proportion as logical faculties are brought into play by it; and hence that logical power is allied, or possibly identical, with the power of grasping more subtle jokes. The jokes which amuse the frequenters of music-halls, Conservatives, and M. Bergson—and which usually deal with accidents, physical defects, mothers-in-law, foreigners, or over-ripe cheese—are usually jokes of the first order. Jokes of the second, and even of the third, order appeal to ordinary well-educated people; jokes

[1] It may be that, like certain remarks about cheese and mothers-in-law (see below), the statement that Scotsmen cannot see jokes is a joke of the first order.—ED.

of higher order require either special ability or a sound logical training on the part of the hearer if the joke is to be appreciated; while jokes of transfinite order presumably only excite the inaudible laughter of the gods.

BIBLIOGRAPHY

ANDREWS, P. B. *A Transfinite Type Theory with Type Variables*. Amsterdam, 1965.

BERNAYS, P. 'Review of Gödel 1944'. *Journal of Symbolic Logic*, 11 (1946), 75–9.

BOLZANO, B. *Paradoxes of the Infinite*, trans. Fr. Prihonsky. London, 1950.

BURALI-FORTI, C. 'Una questione sui numeri transfiniti'. *Rendiconti del Circolo Matematico di Palermo*, 11 (1897), 154–64. Translated in van Heijenoort, 1967, 104–11.

'Sulle classi ben ordinate'. *Rendiconti del Circolo Matematico di Palermo*, 11 (1897a), 260. Translated in van Heijenoort, 1967, 111–2.

CANTOR, G. *Contributions to the Founding of the Theory of Transfinite Numbers*. Trans. P. E. B. Jourdain, Chicago and London, 1915.

Gesammelte Abhandlungen. Ed. E. Zermelo, Berlin, 1932.

CARNAP, R. *The Logical Syntax of Language*. Trans. A. Smeaton, New York and London, 1937.

Introduction to Symbolic Logic and its Applications. Trans. W. H. Meyer and J. Wilkinson, New York, 1958.

CHURCH, A. 'The Richard Paradox'. *American Mathematical Monthly*, 41 (1934), 356–61.

Bibliography

'An Unsolvable Problem of Elementary Number Theory'. *American Journal of Mathematics*, 58 (1936), 345–63.

'Schröder's Anticipation of the Simple Theory of Types'. Preprinted for the members of the Fifth International Congress for the Unity of Science, Cambridge, Mass., 1939, as from *Journal of Unified Science (Erkenntnis)*, 9; 4 pp.

'A Formulation of the Simple Theory of Types'. *Journal of Symbolic Logic*, 5 (1940), 56–68.

Introduction to Mathematical Logic. Vol. I, Princeton, 1956.

CHWISTEK, L. 'Antynomje Logiki Formalnej'. *Przeglad Filozoficzny*, 24 (1921), 164–71.

'Über die Antinomien der Prinzipien der Mathematik'. *Mathematische Zeitschrift*, 14 (1922), 236–43.

The Limits of Science. Trans. H. C. Brodie and A. P. Coleman, New York, 1948.

COPI, I. M. 'The Inconsistency or Redundancy of Principia Mathematica'. *Philosophy and Phenomenological Research*, 11 (1950), 190–9.

'The Burali-Forti Paradox'. *Philosophy of Science*, 25 (1958), 281–6.

DEDEKIND, R. *Was sind und was sollen die Zahlen?* Brunswick, 1888. Trans. W. W. Beman in *Essays on the Theory of Numbers*. Chicago and London, 1901.

'Letter to Kefferstein' (1890). Trans. H. Wang and S. Bauer-Mengelberg in van Heijenoort, 1967, 98–103. Partial translation with commentary in Wang, 1957.

DIXON, A. C. 'On "Well-Ordered" Aggregates'. *Pro-*

ceedings of the London Mathematical Society, 2s. 4 (1906), 18–20.

FARIS, J. A. *Truth-Functional Logic*. London, 1962.

FITCH, F. B. 'The Consistency of the Ramified Principia'. *Journal of Symbolic Logic*, 3 (1938), 140–9.

    Symbolic Logic. New York, 1952.

FRAENKEL, A. A. AND BAR-HILLEL, Y. *Foundations of Set Theory*. Amsterdam: North Holland, 1958.

FREGE, G. *Die Grundlagen der Arithmetik*. Breslau, 1884. Trans. J. L. Austin as *The Foundations of Arithmetic*, Oxford, 1953.

    Grundgesetze der Arithmetik. Jena: Vol. 1, 1893; Vol. 2, 1903.

    Translations from the Philosophical Writings of Gottlob Frege. Eds. P. Geach and M. Black, Oxford, 1952.

    The Basic Laws of Arithmetic, Exposition of the System. Trans. and ed. M. Furth, Berkeley and Los Angeles, 1964.

GALILEO GALILEI. *Dialogues Concerning Two New Sciences*. Evanston and Chicago, 1946.

GÖDEL, K. 'Über formal unentscheidbare Sätze der *Principia Mathematica* und verwandter Systeme I'. *Monatshefte für Mathematik und Physik*, 38 (1931), 173–98. Translated in van Heijenoort, 1967, 592–617.

    'Russell's Mathematical Logic'. *The Philosophy of Bertrand Russell*, ed. P. A. Schilpp, Evanston, Illinois, 1944, 123–53.

GRELLING, K. AND NELSON, L. 'Bemerkungen zu den Paradoxien von Russell und Burali-Forti'. *Abhandlung der Fries'schen Schule*, n.s. 2 (1907–8), 300–24.

'The Logical Paradoxes'. *Mind*, n.s. 45 (1936), 481–6.

HILBERT, D. 'Über das Unendliche'. *Mathematische Annalen*, 92 (1926), 161–90.

HUSSERL, E. *Logische Untersuchungen*. Bd. 1. 2 Aufl., Halle a. S., 1913.

Formale und transzendentale Logik. Halle a. S., 1929.

Formal and Transcendental Logic. Trans. D. Cairns, The Hague, 1969.

KEENE, G. *First-Order Functional Calculus*. London, 1964.

KNEALE, W. AND KNEALE. M. *The Development of Logic*. Oxford, 1962.

KÖNIG, J. 'Über die Grundlagen der Mengenlehre und das Kontinuumproblem'. *Mathematische Annalen*, 61 (1905), 156–60.

KURATOWSKI, C. 'Sur la Notion de l'Ordre dans la Théorie des Ensembles'. *Fundamenta Mathematicae*, 2 (1920), 161–71.

LEIBNIZ, G. W. *Mathematische Schriften*. Ed. C. I. Gerhardt, 7 vols, Hildeshein, 1962.

LEMMON, E. J. *Introduction to Axiomatic Set Theory*. London and New York, 1968.

LEWIS, C. I. AND LANGFORD, C. H. *Symbolic Logic*. New York, 1932.

LORENZEN, P. 'Algebraische und Logistische Untersuchungen über Freie Verbände'. *Journal of Symbolic Logic*, 16 (1951), 81–106.

Einführung in die operative Logik und Mathematik. Berlin, Göttingen and Heidelberg, 1955.

MIRIMANOFF, D. 'Les antinomies de Russell et de

Burali-Forti et le problème fondamental de la théorie des ensembles'. *L'Enseignement Mathematique*, 19 (1917), 37–52.

MONTAGUE, R. 'On the Paradox of Grounded Classes'. *The Journal of Symbolic Logic*, 20 (1955), 140.

MOSTOWSKI, A. 'Thirty Years of Foundational Studies'. *Acta Philosophica Fennica*, Fasc. 17 (1965).

NIDDITCH, P. H. *Propositional Calculus*. London and New York, 1962.

OLIVIER, L. 'Le troisième Congrès international des Mathématiciens'. *Revue Générale des Sciences*, 15 (1904), 961–2.

'La Théorie des Ensembles'. *Revue Générale des Sciences*, 16 (1905), 241–2.

PEANO, G. *Arithmetices Principia, Nova Methodo Exposita*. Turin, 1889. Translated in van Heijenoort, 1967, 85–97.

'Addition'. *Revista de Mathematica*, 8 (1906), 143–57.

POINCARÉ, H. 'Les Mathématiques et la Logique'. *Revue de Métaphysique et de Morale*, 14 (1906), 17–34, 294–317.

The Foundations of Science. Trans. G. B. Halsted, Lancaster, Pa., 1913.

POPPER, K. R. 'Self-reference and Meaning in Ordinary Language'. *Mind*, n.s. 63 (1954), 162–9.

Conjectures and Refutations. London, 1963.

QUINE, W. V. O. 'On the Axiom of Reducibility'. *Mind*, n.s. 45 (1936), 498–500.

Mathematical Logic. New York, 1940.

'Whitehead and the Rise of Modern Logic'. *The Philosophy of Alfred North Whitehead*, ed. P. A. S.

Schilpp, Evanston and Chicago, 1941, 127–63. Reprinted in *The Ways of Paradox*, Cambridge, Mass., 1963.

 From a Logical Point of View. Cambridge, Mass., 1953.

 'Paradox'. *Scientific American*, 206 (1962). Reprinted in *The Ways of Paradox*, Cambridge, Mass., 1963.

 Set Theory and Its Logic. Cambridge, Mass., 1963.

 The Ways of Paradox. New York, 1966a.

 Selected Logic Papers. New York, 1966b.

RAMSEY, F. P. 'The Foundations of Mathematics'. *Proceedings of the London Mathematical Society*, 2 s. 25 (1926), 338–84. Reprinted in Ramsey, 1931, 1–61.

 The Foundations of Mathematics. Ed. R. B. Braithwaite, New York and London, 1931.

RICHARD, J. 'Les Principes des Mathematiques et le Problème des Ensembles'. *Revue Générale des Sciences*, 16 (1905), 541–3. Reprinted in *Acta Mathematica*, 30 (1906), 295–6. Translated in van Heijenoort, 1967, 142–4.

RUSSELL, B. 'Recent Work in the Philosophy of Mathematics'. *International Monthly*, 4 (1901), 83–101. Reprinted as Ch. 5 of *Mysticism and Logic*, London, 1918.

 The Principles of Mathematics. Cambridge, England, 1903; 2nd ed., New York, 1938.

 'Les Paradoxes de la Logique'. *Revue de Métaphysique et de Morale*, 14 (1906a), 627–50.

 'On Some Difficulties in the Theory of Transfinite Numbers and Order Types'. *Proceedings of the London Mathematical Society*, 2s. 4 (1906b), 29–53.

Bibliography

'Mathematical Logic as Based on the Theory of Types'. *American Journal of Mathematics*, 30 (1908), 222–62. Reprinted in *Logic and Knowledge*, ed. R. C. Marsh, London, 1956, 59–102. And in van Heijenoort, 1967, 150–82.

The Philosophy of Mr. B*RTR*ND R*SS*LL. Ed. P. E. B. Jourdain, London and Chicago, 1918a.

'Philosophy of *Logical Atomism*'. *Monist*, 28 (1918b), 495–527; 29 (1919a), 32–63, 190–222, 345–80.

Introduction to Mathematical Philosophy. London and New York, 1919b.

'Introduction'. *Tractatus Logico-Philosophicus* by L. Wittgenstein, London, 1922.

The Philosophy of Bertrand Russell. Ed. P. A. Schilpp. Evanston, Ill., 1944.

Logic and Knowledge. Ed. R. C. Marsh, London, 1956.

RÜSTOW, A. *Der Lügner, Theorie, Geschichte und Auflösung*. Leipzig, 1910.

SCHÜTTE, K. 'Beweistheoretische Untersuchungen der verzweigten Analysis'. *Mathematische Annalen*, 124 (1952), 123–47.

SKOLEM, T. *Abstract Set Theory*. Notre Dame, Indiana, 1962.

TARSKI, A. 'Semantic Conception of Truth'. *Philosophy and Phenomenological Research*, 4 (1944), 341–75. Reprinted in *Readings in Philosophical Analysis*, eds. H. Feigl and W. Sellars, New York, 1949, 52–84.

Logic, Semantics, Metamathematics. Trans. J. H. Woodger, Oxford, 1956.

VAN HEIJENOORT, J. *From Frege to Gödel, A Source*

Bibliography

Book in Mathematical Logic, 1879–1931. Cambridge, Mass., 1967.

WANG, H. 'A Theory of Constructive Types'. *Methodos*, 1 (1950), 374–84.

'The Formalization of Mathematics'. *The Journal of Symbolic Logic*, 19 (1954), 241–66.

'The Axiomatization of Arithmetic'. *Journal of Symbolic Logic*, 22 (1957), 145–58.

WHITEHEAD, A. N. AND RUSSELL, B. *Principia Mathematica*. Cambridge, England, Vol. 1, 1910, 2nd ed., 1925; Vol. 2, 1912, 2nd ed., 1927; Vol. 3, 1913, 2nd ed., 1927.

WIENER, N. 'A Simplification of the Logic of Relations'. *Proceedings of the Cambridge Philosophical Society*, 17 (1912–4), 387–90.

WITTGENSTEIN, L. *Tractatus Logico-Philosophicus*. London, 1922.

YUTING, S. 'Paradox of the Class of All Grounded Classes'. *Journal of Symbolic Logic*, 18 (1953), 114.

ZERMELO, E. 'Neuer Beweis für die Möglichkeit einer Wohlordnung'. *Mathematische Annalen*, 65 (1908a), 107–128. Trans. S. Bauer-Mengelberg in van Heijenoort, 1967, 183–98.

'Untersuchungen über die Grundlagen der Mengenlehre I'. *Mathematische Annalen*, 65 (1908b), 261–81. Trans. S. Bauer-Mengelberg in van Heijenoort, 1967, 199–215.

INDEX

127

Index